D1436113

BEER
IN SO MANY WORDS

BEER
IN SO MANY WORDS

THE BEST WRITING
ON THE GREATEST DRINK

**Edited by
Adrian Tierney-Jones**

SAFE HAVEN

in association with

THE
HOMEWOOD
·PRESS·

First published 2016 by
Safe Haven Books Ltd
12 Chinnocks Wharf
42 Narrow Street
London E14 8DJ
www.safehavenbooks.co.uk

in association with
The Homewood Press
2 Chene Mews
St Albans AL3 5QF

A catalogue record for this book is available from the British Library.

ISBN 978 0 993291 1 1

10 9 8 7 6 5 4 3 2 1

2020 2019 2018 2017 2016

Typeset in Brandon and Mrs Eaves by SX Composing DTP, Rayleigh, Essex
Printed and bound by CPI Group (UK) Ltd, Croydon CR0 4YY

CONTENTS

3   Beer People   91

4 The Brewing of Beer 123

5 Beer Journeys 157

INTRODUCTION

God has a brown voice, as soft and full as beer.

Anne Sexton

The beer in the glass: the long cool liquid which might gleam like sunlight and lift the spirits. Or it might settle in a chalice-like vessel reminiscent of something out of Camelot, broody and moody like a knight plotting revenge. That's what beer writing is about - this wonderful liquid that refreshes, that sparks conversation with friends and strangers, or maybe aids contemplation in the company of a book or a favoured piece of music.

Beer writing is also about the people who make it and drink it (and sometimes sell it); it is about its history, its place in a nation's self-regard; it is about landscape and travel, and where you're going and where you've been; it is about its philosophy, its business, its dynamics, its culture, its language, and above all the space it's taken in human life since someone in the Middle East a few thousand years ago thought that the combination of crushed dried barley and water and what we know as fermentation made for a pretty damn fine drink.

Beer writing, like film writing, wine writing, sports writing and music writing (of which I did a fair bit of the latter in my youth), encompasses a whole universe of subjects, and some of the best writers on drink and drinking (and food) inhabit its hallowed spheres. It's also been around a long time. In *The Epic of Gilgamesh*, believed to be one of the earliest works of literature to survive, beer is one of the ways in which the sacred prostitute Shamhat turns the formerly wild man Enkidu (originally created from clay and saliva by the gods) into a human. Meanwhile Plato hit the nail on the head when he wrote, "He was a wise man who invented beer". Though I suspect what he had in his glass down at the Old Temple and Pantheon was a bit different from what I normally have in mine.

Chaucer probably liked the odd noggin, though his pilgrims would have called it ale and thought the hop a pernicious weed fit for foreigners. Shakespeare ditto, who had one of his characters say that they "would give all my fame for a pot of ale and safety". Dr Johnson, Napoleon Bonaparte, Charles Dickens, Robert Louis Stevenson, Kaiser Wilhelm II, Thomas Hardy, A.E. Housman and James Joyce: they all had something to say about beer; words that are worth conserving.

They were not beer writers in the modern, modish sense of the term, but they wrote about beer that could get a parched throat anticipating a flood, and a flurry of amber liquid, spiked with hops, softened by malt: a drink that refreshes and perks up the mind. As the years of the 20th century continued to unfold they were joined by the likes of Patrick Leigh Fermor, Patrick Hamilton, Ernest Hemingway, Graham Swift and Graham Greene, all of whom made space for beer in their work. "When I die," wrote J.P. Donleavy in *The Ginger Man*, "I want to decompose in a barrel of porter and have it served in all the pubs in Dublin."

Now let's meet a modern beer writer. Here is a man or woman who cares about and drinks deeply of beer, who dares to ask questions and task themselves to discover the rich vein of knowledge that flows through the world of beer. The beer writer looks at the world through the bottom of a glass, through the top of a tap takeover (or corporate ram-raid if they so wish); they spin a yarn, make the hard yards, girdle the globe or just pop into their local with the intention of hearing tales and re-telling them in their own way.

In this anthology of beer writing (or writings on beer if you so prefer) I have tried to bring together and link up these two strands; to leaven the contemporary with the historical; to ally the long read, the observation from the bar-room and the analytical with the passing moment, the brief tale, the epigram that once said vanishes like a rainbow unless it is caught in print (or online).

Beer has a history: it has made its mark on civilisations and culture and, if we look at the emergence of India Pale Ale in the 19th century, can perhaps even call itself a driver of progress. With India Pale Ale we have to be aware of the clash between history and legend, and beer historian Martyn Cornell, more than most, has been able to sift out the facts from the fiction, as his article on how the big storm (perhaps) helped India Pale Ale become the beer of Victorian England, demonstrates.

Nearer to our time, Ray Bailey and Jessica Boak tell the fascinating tale of Becky's Dive, an early pioneer of a pub selling a wide variety of cask beers. Then there is travel, whether it's Will Hawkes dissecting the competing beer styles of Düsseldorf and Cologne for the *Washington Post*, George Borrow writing about various Welsh beers on his travels, or *All About Beer*'s John Holl being wry and spry about his short stay in a Las Vegas hotel devoted to Bud Light.

Beer writing is also about the people who make the beer: the brewer, both he and she, who gets up in the morning and rubs their hands with anticipation at the joy they are going to conjure up in the brewery that day. However, it's not just about the people who push the buttons or empty the mash tuns or put in the hops, it's also about the likes of Keith Villa, in Stan Hieronymous's masterful profile. He is the brewer who designed Blue Moon, one of the most successful modern beers in the USA.

Then there are the men and the women who sit in the pub, filtering their lives through its prism. It might be Adam, whom award-winning Edinburgh-based beer writer Richard Taylor has beautifully and elegantly written about, or it could be the effusive wordsmith or the pub poet Alastair Gilmour introduces us to.

Talking of the pub brings us to perhaps some of the most famous words ever written about this much-loved and put-upon institution: "The Moon Under Water" was a column George Orwell wrote in the *Evening Standard* in 1946, an elegiac and elegant motet on his ideal pub. What would your favourite be? Mine is the one where beer, ambience, sociability, conversation and comfort co-exist, which I suspect is quite close to Orwell's perfect place. Orwell is also channelled by Ian Nairn's eulogy on the country pub, and Pete Brown's elegiac words on the pub that's about to become a Wetherspoon's. Of course, beer is drunk in other places around the world besides the pub, and I would like to think that my observations of Prague's famous brewpub U Fleků offer a few insights into a different drinking culture.

Writing about how beer tastes, how it's drunk and how it continues to enthrall people through the ages, is also an integral part of beer writing. Those that pursue this particular avenue can be philosophers, cheerleaders for beer, critics, analysts, observers and reporters. This includes such writers as Roger Protz (who once lectured on beer at the Smithsonian in Washington DC), American author Tom Acitelli, whose book *The Audacity of Hops* is an outstanding narrative of the US craft beer revolution, and the late great Michael Jackson ("the gloveless one", as he liked to say), who back in the 1970s laid down the template for modern beer writing.

Part of that template was visiting breweries, seeing where the beer was made and talking to the people who made it, right across the world. For instance, the award-winning Breandán Kearney tells the tale of Brouwerij De Ranke, while back in the 19th century novelist Sir Walter Besant evokes a then contemporary London brewery, and the beers it made.

Writing about food and beer and how they all go together is a comparatively recent activity, though there were a couple of cookbooks in the 1950s and 60s, but three of the best beer writers on the subject are Lucy Saunders, Lisa Morrison and

Sue Nowak, all of whose work appears here. And if you fancy having a go at some beer cuisine in the kitchen, try your hand at Garrett Oliver's Indian-spiced crab cakes.

Beer writing? It's a discipline, an exercise, a profession, an art that covers the universe and beyond. I hope this anthology will reveal some of that world to you the reader (and I suspect beer drinker). Which reminds me: the sun's over the yard arm, the pub in the next street has opened its doors, and I think it's time for a beer. What's yours?

Adrian Tierney-Jones
September 2016

The Taste

1

THE TASTE OF BEER

"Did you ever taste beer?"
"I had a sip of it once," said the servant.
"Here's a state of things!" cried Mr Swiveller,
raising his eyes to the ceiling.
"She never tasted it — it can't be tasted in a sip!"

Charles Dickens, *The Old Curiosity Shop*

A Pleasure That Has Never Failed Me

Graham Greene

Alcohol began to appeal to me in the innocent form of bitter beer. I was offered beer first by Lubbock, my riding master, whom I visited one evening in summer. I hated the taste and drank it down with an effort to prove my manliness, and yet some days later, on a long country walk with Raymond, the memory of the taste came back to taunt my thirst. We stopped at an inn for bread and cheese, and I drank bitter for the second time and enjoyed the taste with a pleasure that has never failed me since.

A Sort of Life, 1971

Ballantine Ale

Ernest Hemingway

Bob Benchley first introduced me to Ballantine Ale. It has been a good companion ever since.

You have to work hard to deserve it. But I would rather have a bottle of Ballantine Ale than any other drink after fighting a really big fish. When something has been taken out of you by strenuous exercise Ballantine puts it back in.

We keep it iced in the bait box with chunks of ice packed around it. And you ought to taste it on a hot day when you have worked a big marlin because there were sharks after him.

You are tired all the way through. The fish is landed untouched by sharks and you have a bottle of Ballantine cold in your hand and drink it cool, light, and full-bodied, so it tastes good long after you have swallowed it. That's the test of an ale with me: whether it tastes as good afterwards as when it's going down. Ballantine does.

1951

ENLIGHTEN THE DARKNESS
OF THE PEOPLE

A Drinker

But, although beer is more popular than it used to be it is still not popular enough. And so it is incumbent upon all true amateurs of beer to take the necessary steps to enlighten the darkness of the people. It is incumbent upon them to spread knowledge about beer and insist upon getting beer when they are lunching and dining. When taking luncheon in a club on Piccadilly the other day I called for a tankard of bitter. The wine waiter brought it and I then asked what brand it was.

That waiter had been bringing members beer for years; yet he did not know what brand of beer he had been giving them and, presumably, none of them had thought to ask. I called the head steward and asked him the same question. He was not certain but he rather thought it was so-and-so's beer. Neither the head steward nor the wine waiter in that expensive London club knew the first thing about beer; a drink that was being used by a large number of members every day. Had I asked either of them about the wines in their cellars they would have furnished me with very complete information and probably with a considered opinion of the merits of the wine concerned. But beer! Well, it's just beer, and you can have it on draught or out of a bottle and that is all they know about it.

Let the army of amateurs of beer inquire at their clubs what brands of beer are available and let them then inquire why those brands are available and why other brands are not available. Let them try to discover who decided what brand to order and upon what basis he came to his decision. It will exercise their staffs and committees and make them see that the choice of beer is worthy of consideration.

A Book About Beer, 1934

REFRESHING LIKE TRUTH ITSELF

Dale Jacquette

Oh, Jerusalem, Jerusalem! Or rather, oh, Zundert, oh, Zundert!
Vincent van Gogh, Letter to Theo, 7/8 February 1877

The quest for a satisfying glass of beer can be understand as a metaphor for a deeper thirst for authenticity. A properly poured glass, served at the right temperature, with just the right balance of hops and malted barley, refreshing and fortifying, like truth itself, is something pure and worth pursing for its own sake.

I speak not of beer in cans or bottles, but of beer fresh from the barrel or keg. It should be draft beer hand pumped into a glass and encouraged to build a creamy head that spills over the rim and comes to the table as a potable work of fine art as noble as any our civilisation has produced. The virtues of beer must be contrasted on purely aesthetic grounds with those of wine, distilled liquors, and the moral disgrace of total abstinence. The enjoyment of beer is an ancient democratic, yea, proletarian pleasure that at its best reflects the natural products of the harvest handcrafted to bring their full potential to fruition. The right beer, the best, most delicious, noble and rewarding beer, is nevertheless as elusive as ultimate philosophical truth, and context and state of mind have as much to do with the experiences as the chemical composition of the wort and the process and natural history of its fermentation.

To seek a perfect beer is to open all one's epistemic resources to new discoveries in much the same way as an explorer setting forth to find uncharted islands. There is much to learn, much to savour, and much to avoid as dangerous and unpalatable, where an adventurous discriminating palate is one's only guide.

from "Thirst for Authenticity: An Aesthetics of the Brewer's Art", *in Beer and Philosophy: The Unexamined Beer Isn't Worth Drinking*, 2007

BREWED THROUGH A HORSE

Mike Royko

The American beer industry answers its critics by saying it gives us the kind of beer we really want.

Oh yeah?

This weekend I ran a beer-tasting session in which 11 people sampled 22 beers.

The beers included the biggest selling American brands, imports from eight countries, and a few small-town American breweries that sell mostly in their own areas. The tasters, drinking from unmarked glasses, rated each beer from one point (barely drinkable) to five points (great). The most points a beer could have received was 55. The least was 11. Here are the results:

Wurzburger (Germany):	46.5
Bass Ale (England):	45
Point Special (Stevens Point, Wisc):	45
Heineken's (Holland):	36.5
Old Timer's (Eau Claire, Wisc):	35.5
Zywiec (Poland):	34.5
Löwenbrau (Germany):	29.5
Huber Premium (Monroe, Wisc):	29.5
Kirin (Japan):	29
Stroh's (US):	26
Barrel of Beer (Monroe, Wisc):	26
Miller's (US):	26
Meister Brau (US):	25.5
Hamm's (US):	25.5
Ringnes (Norway):	23.5
Pilsner Urquell (Czechoslovakia):	23
Pickett's (Dubuque, Iowa):	22.5
Old Chicago (Chicago):	22.5
Carta Blanca (Mexico):	21.5
Old Milwaukee (US):	20.5
Schlitz (US):	18.5
Budweiser (US):	13

As you can see, clustered at the top were nine beers that didn't include any of the major American brands. And a distant last were our two biggest TV braggarts.

The whole thing was rigged, some patriotic beer drinker is saying. I rigged it because I've said that America's beer tastes as if it is brewed through a horse, and I wanted to find a panel of tasters who would agree with me.

That isn't so. The panel consisted of men and women who didn't know what beers they were tasting. Some of them usually drink only American popular brands. Others drink foreign and domestics. A few seldom drink beer at all, and a few others drink it regularly. They included young people and middle-aged people. Their ethnicity ranged from German to Polish to Bohemian to Irish to Norwegian to Jewish to WASP. To keep their taste buds alert, a variety of snacks were provided, including fresh Augusta rye bread, liverwurst, Polish sausage, potato chips, dill pickles, pigs feet, and other haute cuisine. To show how legit the testing was, I didn't take part. My job was to wash glasses and break up fights.

If anything, the imported beers were at a disadvantage. Beer loses flavour if it is on the shelf too long. And foreign beers must be shipped a long way and they'd don't turn over in the stores as quickly as the popular American brands.

This could explain why Pilsner Urquell — considered by most brewing masters to be the world's finest — did so poorly. Pilsner Urquell, from the world's oldest brewery, is so good that it is the leading import of Germans.

As the tasters wrote down the points for each beer, they also jotted some observations. Among the comments about Wurzburger, the top scorer, were: "full rich flavour and no aftertaste"; "solid taste"; "very good"; "I could drink a lot more". About Point Special, which is brewed about 220 miles north of Chicago, they said: "great flavour and great beer smell"; "light and lovely and I could drink it all night"; "smooth"; "could drink a lot of it".

Ah, but the things they said about those beers that are the subjects of huge, spectacular TV commercials. After the samples of Schlitz were brought around, I didn't notice anybody grabbing for any gusto. A few people grabbed for potato chips to get rid of the taste. Among their notations were: "this beer is tired"; "weak"; "nasty", and "ugh". Maybe at the ad agency it is gospel that when you say Budweiser, you've said it all. But my backyard beer tasters had a few additional comments about Bud: "a picnic beer smell"; "lousy"; "Alka Seltzer"; "sweet and weak"; "yeccch".

Schlitz and Bud are free to use any of the above comments as testimonials, or in their next commercials. It might be fun to see one of those dashing actors on a sailing ship downing a can of beer and instead of grabbing for gusto, grabbing his stomach and yelling: "Yeecch!"

Chicago Evening News, July 1973

CRAFT BEER IS HAVING A CHARDONNAY MOMENT

Tom Acitelli

US beer is about to change forever stylistically — just like wine did 50 years ago.

It has been more than 50 years since home-appliance heir Fritz Maytag rescued the flailing Anchor Brewing Co. of San Francisco and unwittingly spawned the modern American craft beer movement. From that one brewery that Mr Maytag saved in 1965 — it was the last of its kind then — more than 3,500 craft breweries have grown up. Yet, despite titanic growth in the sector, these smaller breweries have amassed a national sales-market share of around just 15 percent.

The vast majority of US beer drinkers still knock back Bud, Miller Lite and their macro brethren. Is there any hope that more flavourful India pale ales, Oktoberfests and stouts will dethrone them?

There is. It can be found in the example of American fine wine.

Pink Chablis: The Wine Drinker's Bud Light

Fifty years ago, most of the wine produced in the US, never mind sold, was made from lower-end grapes such as Salvador, Carignan and Alicante Bouschet. These were prized less for their taste than for their ability to ferment fast and undergird the coarser, stronger wines preferred by most Americans who drank wine. Plus, they grew pretty much anywhere. In 1961, Merlot grapes covered barely 50 acres of California wine country; Carignan covered 25,000.

If consumers wanted rounder, drier wines made from the likes of Chardonnay and Cabernet Sauvignon, they invariably bought French — or, in a pinch, Italian. A small handful of US wineries made bottles from grapes like that, but their sales were minuscule.

No, the American wine benchmark was Pink Chablis, a wine that E. & J. Gallo, the nation's biggest winery, introduced in 1965. Gallo never listed the grapes used, and the concoction tasted like a cross between Kool-Aid and spiked punch. It sold phenomenally.

Then, the year after Gallo foisted Pink Chablis on the public, Robert Mondavi started his eponymous winery, the first significant new one in Napa Valley since Prohibition, and things began to change. The indefatigably gregarious Mondavi, who died in 2008, proved a remarkable salesman for higher-quality wine in general, never mind his own brands, which included a highly acclaimed Cabernet Sauvignon.

A shift in national taste helped him immensely. For a variety of reasons, including a generational changeover — those rebellious baby boomers didn't care for the drinks of their parents — and a rise in the number of wineries specializing in European styles such as Cabernet Sauvignon, Americans started drinking more drier, finer wines and far fewer of the ones made from Carignan and its ilk.

A decades-long preference reversed itself. Wineries throughout the land saw the sales writing on the wall and gradually shifted their production.

Newcomers never even considered making anything else.

A thumping victory over the long-hegemonic French in a 1976 blind tasting that came to be called the Judgement of Paris only solidified the rise of American fine wine. As did a bounce in wine coverage among trade and consumer media: A *New York Times* reporter named Frank Prial became the newspaper's first regular wine critic in 1972, for instance, and *Wine Spectator*, Wine Enthusiast and *Wine Advocate* all launched before the decade's end.

Today, it seems as if the likes of Merlot and Barolo have always dominated the US wine marketplace — which, incidentally, has become the biggest in the world, belting the French from that perch in 2014. Yet a grape such as Chardonnay was not even among the top five most-grown wine grapes in California in the early 1970s. (Carignan was.) Now Chardonnay is the most popular wine style in the US.

If You Can't Beat 'Em, Buy 'Em

A similar taste shift is under way in beer. American craft beer sales volume grew annually nearly 18 percent in 2014, according to the Brewers Association trade group. That was well ahead of the anaemic 0.5 percent growth of beer sales overall.

The last time craft beer grew this steadily was in the 1990s. The sector went bust toward the end of that decade as too many entrants flooded the market with too much iffy beer. Around one-third of the craft breweries in the US closed.

There is no sign of such a slowdown this time. The quality is uniformly good, and the support is there: in trade, consumer, and social media; in massive festivals (the Great American Beer Festival in Denver every autumn is the world's biggest beer-tasting festival); even in the White House – President Obama in 2011 became the first president to homebrew there when staff made an ale flavoured with honey from a hive on the mansion's grounds (and using a kit the president bought himself).

Make no mistake: craft beer faces huge challenges. The rising price of hops, beer's all-important bittering agent, has many smaller players concerned. The vast majority of craft brewers are those smaller players, too, churning out fewer than 15,000 barrels a year. Their margins are often razor-thin.

There has also been a lot of infighting between craft brewers lately, including legally, over things such as images and slogans. Accusations that some craft brewers were illegally paying Massachusetts bar owners to carry their beers rocked the normally collegial New England craft beer scene earlier this year.

Finally, Big Beer operations have adopted an "If you can't beat 'em, buy 'em" approach to a craft beer sector they've long either ignored or clumsily imitated (see Coors' Blue Moon). Anheuser-Busch InBev, the nation's biggest brewer, bought Chicago's Goose Island in 2011, Bend, Oregon's 10 Barrel and Long Island's Blue Point in 2014, and Seattle's Elysian and Los Angeles's Golden Road this year. Just this summer, MillerCoors acquired a majority stake in St Archer's out of

San Diego, and Lagunitas, the fastest-growing craft brewery in the US, signed a 50-50 partnership with Heineken.

That trend in itself, though, whatever it might mean for the industry, shows where beer is headed taste-wise in America. Lagunitas' founder and chief, Tony Magee, bragged on social media that his deal with the much larger Heineken only means more Lagunitas IPAs et al on the shelves in more places.

Far from the end of craft beer, the recent Big Beer rigmarole and craft infighting, not to mention the rapid expansion of some craft operations, is the salvation for craft beer stylistically. It's all going to get so much tastier from here on out for consumers.

Budweiser and Miller Lite appear destined to be shunted to the sides of the beer aisle — and sooner than many think. It's taking a while — more than half a century now — but just look at Chardonnay.

www.foodrepublic.com, November 2015

A Taste Of Garlic Or Onions

The first Brewers' National Exhibition and Market, London

The various exhibits of beers, wines and spirits were arranged in a separate portion of the hall, to which a charge of admission of sixpence each person was made. These so-called tasting stalls were in several instances elaborately and artistically fitted up, and their different occupiers competed with each other in their eagerness in offering samples to the throngs who continually passed by. In this department there were exhibits of both German and English beer; one exhibitor of American lager was entered in the catalogue but we failed to find his stand. We have no desire to speak disrespectfully of German beer, but the samples offered to the public were such as we feel sure will never replace home-brewed beer in this country; the thinness on the palate, the absence of all flavour of malt extract, the artificial aeration, the peculiar taste described by most of the public as resembling garlic or onions, are all characteristics which, however agreeable to the German taste, will take a long time to be acclimatised here; when such beers are offered at prices ranging from 2s to 3s per gallon, we think English brewers have not much to fear from competition from that quarter, at all events so far as our home trade is concerned.

Brewers' Guardian, October 1879

LONG DRAUGHTS WITH AN OPEN THROAT

Maurice Healy

Beer is the most English drink of all. It takes many forms; in Germany they prefer it in the shape of *lager*; in England, some prefer it mild and some prefer it bitter; some prefer draught and some prefer bottled. All are good. I consider that my education was sadly neglected, in that I never tasted beer until the year 1927. I was ready for it; for I have always thought that the best Cheddar cheese is that which has a strong beery flavour. But whenever I was offered a glass of beer I sipped it nervously, and was nearly sick. Then I found myself on one scorching summer's day walking down the main street of Cologne. All around me were shops and restaurants where smiling waiters were bringing to their customers tall beakers of ice-cold *lager*, with a frost forming on the outside of the glass. I could resist it no longer; I ordered one for myself; and when it arrived I *opened my throat and swilled it down*. And then I knew how good beer could be. Of course, the fault had been in myself; I had tried to drink beer the way one should drink wine: by sipping it. And there are few things so revolting as sipped beer. But let it go down your throat "as suds go down the sink," and you will quickly realise that this is a true friend, to be admitted to your most secret counsels. Long draughts with an open throat are the secret.

Although I regularly drink *lager* in Germany (or used to, when that country was fit to visit), I rarely drink English draught ale. This does not come from pride or want of appreciation of its excellence; there is a slightly soapy flavour that I meet too often in it. There are a few of the London ales that I care for: Watney's, perhaps, coming first, although there is a house of call near Belgrave Square kept by an old friend of mine where I drink Fuller's with great pleasure. But I think that for really good beer you must go north of the Trent. And I do not refer to Burton; I have drunk delicious brews of Bass and Worthington and Ind Coope; but I have also drunk them when they were not so good. Offilers of Derby I have always found agreeable and sometimes worthy of still higher praise; Stone's of Sheffield brew a steady, good ale; the John Smith (Tadcaster) Brewery I have also found very reliable; and it is a matter of regret to me that I have never had the opportunity of trying Lancashire ales, which presumably have helped to make the Lancashire Fusiliers what they are; and what higher praise could be given? Younger's is the only beer from north of the border that I know and I grudge it no compliment. Of course, I am at the moment speaking of draught and bottled ale; for Gordon's *lager* is in my opinion as good as any German competitor, if not better. The Wrexham *lager* is good also; but I confess that I do not like the taste of Barclay's. This need not worry the brewers, for I do not like the flavour of Guinness either; but I cannot believe that there could be a consensus of good opinion about an inferior product as there is about Guinness.

Beer ought to be given greater honour in England; it is an insufferable thing that certain restaurants and hotels should deny it a place at honourable tables. Take that most hospitable and elegant of countries, Sweden. Every dinner of ceremony begins with beer and goes onto wine. A tankard of ale ought to be a recognised decoration of the proudest banquet; and by the way, ale ought to be drunk out of a tankard: glasses seem an effeminate dress for it. Perhaps we take comfort from the fact that many of those that banished honest English beer from their tables are at the moment banished from those tables themselves; and in their absence a better tradition may grow up.

Slay Me with Flagons, 1940

THE BEST BEERS OF OUR LIVES

Ian Nairn

It may be the fifty-ninth second of the fifty-ninth minute after eleven o'clock, but I think there is now a chance of saving what remains of draught beer in Britain. CAMRA, the Campaign for Real Ale, had 1,800 members a year ago; it now has 18,000, including me. Theakston's of Masham have just bought the Carlisle State brewery, which will shake up the big brewers round there, for all that they own no pub in Cumberland: the news will filter through from the clubs and free houses. The tiny Selby Brewery, reopened in 1972 after 18 years, will be sitting on a goldmine when the coalfield opens up. And many people are travelling many miles to Suffolk not only for sea air but to drink Adnams bitter. But Melbourn's of Stamford stopped brewing last month, Gray's of Chelmsford later this year. There isn't much time left.

Why bother? Think of it in terms of wine. True draught bitter in Britain is in its way as good as the best of claret or hock – without the snobbery or the expense. And unlike good wine, it doesn't exist anywhere else. Because of the hops we use and the way we brew, British beer is unique. German and Swiss beer is halfway there – by that I don't mean it is half as good, simply that British beer is a different animal: the rest of the world drinks lager. Lager can be very good indeed; but if you want to look at a giraffe it is useless for even the best zoo to provide an ocelot.

Think further: to extinguish a local flavour, which is what has happened a hundred times in the last three years, is like abolishing the Beaujolais: after all, it's red and alcoholic, might as well make it in Eurocity to an agreed Common Market recipe. The profits would be enormous, and the peasants wouldn't know the difference . . . but the peasants are fighting back.

There are two main points at issue. One is keg versus draught beer; the second is the arbitrary extinction of local flavours in favour of a "national brew" – like putting a spire on to York Minster to make it more like Salisbury. Dependent on each is a subsidiary but important point. On draught beer, the question of by what system it is served. On the takeover by the "big six" – Allied, Bass-Charrington, Courage/John Smith, Watney-Truman, Whitbread (together they own almost 60% of British pubs) – the question of closing pubs once they have a virtual monopoly. This has happened on a large scale in Norfolk, under Watney's. They eventually took over all three of the Norwich breweries and have in the cause of rationalisation left several villages, like Stiffkey, without a single pub.

But the big issue is keg versus draught. Keg is dead, sterilised at the brewery; draught is live, still working as you drink it – organic food indeed. The difference in taste is easy to explain: keg acts in two dimensions, with a flavour as it passes the teeth and tongue. Draught acts in three, and with luck has first a bouquet, like Adnams' – the wine parallels are apt – then an immediate flavour and an explosion at the back of the mouth, as though the odd system of palate and uvula had suddenly become a sounding-board. To switch similes, it is something like the difference between Danish Blue and a ripe old Roquefort.

This is not just a fad, but a vital difference. What *could* become a fad is the arguments which are now being spelt out at length over the way to serve draught beer. The simplest way, no doubt, is straight out of the barrel through the tap. This depends on whether you have a room cold enough (around $55°F$) to do this: some unimproved pubs have just that, at the back of the bar, though they are hard to find. Otherwise it comes from the cellar, via hand-pumps – mostly in the North – or systems which use carbon dioxide as the motive power.

This last, called top pressure, is what is causing the trouble. Ind Coope were I think the first to introduce it generally in "Super-draught" – now called Special Bitter, not from any legal pressures but simply because they wanted a change of name. I wonder how much that put on the price of a pint, on account of all the alterations needed. The trouble is that beer generates its own CO_2; if too much is injected artificially it can carbonate draught beer to the point where it tastes like keg.

Hence the to-and-fro. CAMRA is, understandably, having growing pains; but it would be a Pyrrhic victory to win the top pressure battle and lose the draught beer war.

Because, with the big six, a war it seems to be. God knows why, unless this truly is the unacceptable face of capitalism — i.e. not only to make profits, which few brewers can fail to do, but to have to make much bigger profits than last year. In pursuit of that, they have gobbled and been gobbled. Three little stories in my own drinking experience, which only goes back 20 years, as I was an abstemious lad until I got the taste.

One. Westerham Ales. Kent; Churchill country. A lovely pint where you could smell the hops half an inch above the beer. Westerham was gobbled by Taylor Walker (as also were Chesham and Brackley) and TW in turn by Ind Coope. The brewery is still there: the beer isn't.

Two. Phipps of Northampton. Perhaps the saddest case of all. In the mid-sixties, going north from London, we would hold out until a Phipps house; both ordinary and best provided a marvellous drink — one of the best tests of any good brewery. Came Watney's. Disappeared Phipps, as a special flavour. This was doubly sad because Phipps is a famous name in Northampton: there is even a Victorian suburb called Phippsville. As well pull down Northampton market place; as it happens the planners are trying quite hard to do just that. Thanks, all; but don't expect me to remember you in my will — or to drink anything but Guinness in a Watney's/Phipps pub.

Three. Smith's of Oundle — a decent country pint, around 1965; a bit like Ruddles, which still thrives next door brewing from Oakham, Rutland. Well now, Smith's was swallowed by Warwick's of Newark, a bad idea. And Warwick's in turn was swallowed by Barnsley Bitter, a good idea — at the time. But now Courage/John Smith have not only swallowed Barnsley Bitter but propose to close it in 1976. Remember the name;

it was a famous brew which provoked the same kind of loyalty as Fed. Special (the club-only beer) in the north-east and Ansell's Mild in the Midlands. If there is a stand-up fight that is here the crunch will come.

The regional differences still exist. In the course of my inquiries, as they say in the police courts, I encountered five stupendous pints, the kind that would make you go straight back to the bar, if a stranger, and say what is this called? Four were traditional shire brews, if I can call them that: bitter, hoppy in the nose and at the back of the mouth. Adnams' of Southwold, Theakston's of Masham – who also brew Old Peculier, which is what Guinness would taste like if they made barley wine. Batham's of Brierley Hill, in the Black Country, which is now one of the best places in Britain for good beer. And Yates and Jackson of Lancaster, a firm which often doesn't even bother to announce its name over the pub door: the reputation is enough.

The fifth came from an apparently nondescript roadblock – Horndean on the A3 between Petersfield and Portsmouth. The roadside brewery is Gale's, the taste both bitter and sweet: they try very hard with their country wines, like elderberry, and the nearest I can get to the flavour is to say that it is honeyed without being cloying. Which oddly enough is the impression left by Stone's of Sheffield – taken over by Bass Charrington but so far left in peace. "If they ever stopped it, there'd be a revolution," said a former colleague whose girth was also nurtured on Hancock's of Cardiff and who may now, being sent off to govern the *Western Mail*, be regretting its replacement by a pint of (Bass Charrington again) Welsh Brewers.

To these you can add Wadworth's of Devizes, Boddington's of Manchester – whose shareholders resisted a takeover in 1971, God bless 'em – Jennings of Cockermouth brewing up against the Castle walls, who did the same last year, Marston's of Burton who are prepared to buy up beer pumps to re-convert pubs to the old heave-ho (and beware their Pedigree: it is smooth but deceptively strong), Mansfield Ales of the creamy pint, King & Barnes of the real Sussex bitter, Shepheard Neame of Faversham, Kent, Ridley's of Chelmsford, and perhaps 50 others. If they are not all mentioned it is due to lack of space, not lack of goodwill; I could recite them in my sleep.

It should be Ridley's and Gray's of Chelmsford: the county town of Essex now has an almost unique situation whereby there are two independent breweries producing good beer with completely different flavours. For a few more months only; as I said, Gray's will close before the end of the year. So, Londoners, head out east quick. To the Cock at Ongar, for example: the nearest Gray's house I know. Beer from the wood, without artifice – the barrel is nudging the bartender. No head, no zip-zap brilliance, and it tastes marvellous.

Central London is a beer-drinker's desert. West London is a good idea, with Young's of Wandsworth and Fuller's of Chiswick – with Watney's Mortlake brewery in between for a bit of the other. The Thames Valley is well off – Brakspear of Henley, Morland of Abingdon. Norfolk and Devon have no independent breweries, but Suffolk has two and Dorset has four, plus Mrs Pardoe's home-brew at Netherton. West Yorkshire is running out of independent ale, Lancashire can still offer the choice.

The choice. As a consumer that's all I ask. You can brew bland brand X until it runs out of your conditioned reflexes, as long as you give me the choice. Otherwise I'll drink Guinness, and there may be tens of thousands with the same calibre of unsatisfied throat. Join the Deep Throat men – to use the kind of slogan that has cost consumers millions of pounds on their real pints in advertising campaigns to propagate false pints. Would you be a Shallow Throat? – for shame.

Now, how can they be shamed? The Adnams's need no admonition, the Okells — of the Isle of Man, and good stuff — no obloquy. Hall & Woodhouse of Blandford — Badger Ales — don't need badgering. All these, and about 50 more, are brewing beer because they want to. But for the rest, and the beer-deserts, what can be done? Quite a lot.

A. To at least two of the big six: think again. Whitbread's are not now thinking of closing many of the breweries under their "umbrella" — which many consumers might well liken to a free-fall parachute without a ripcord. Why not go a bit further, and reverse the idle nationwide designation of Trophy Bitter? Idle, because, thank God, Trophy is *not* the same from place to place. In Kent it still resembles Fremlin's, in Lancashire it tastes like Duttons. This, if we can get it through the thickheads who wouldn't know Worthington White Shield from Watney's Red, could be a financial advantage apart from anything else.

Second, Courage's. You still brew good beer, and it still tastes different. If it comes from Reading (ex-Simonds) it can be superb. If it comes from Bristol (ex-George's) it is one of the cheapest decent pints of draught in Britain. Yet Courage want to close both by 1980, if they can find a site for a new brewery handy to the M4. Think again, and don't disguise, advertise — *vive la difference*.

B. Free houses. Time was when this was almost a guarantee of genuine draught Bass or Worthington. Now, more often than not, it is a guarantee that you will find as many kinds of keg beer as the landlord can cram into one bar-top. Landlord, cram in just one more — the best local draught bitter you can find.

Trust Houses Forte are in an exceptionally good position to do this: they cover the country, and local firms are allowed to tender. So there is Adnams' in the Brudenell in Aldeburgh. And the splendid Swiss landlord of the four-star Shakespeare at Stratford — whose Worthington Best Bitter was already a good idea — not only installed Donnington Ales, from the prettiest brewery in England, in a Cotswold valley near Stow-on-the-Wold, but also installed hand-pumps to serve it properly. Trust Houses Forte could make a marvellous thing out of this. They have, for example, a splendid small hotel at Peaslake, in the Surrey Hills west of Dorking. King & Barnes brew good stuff at Horsham, 5 miles away, but you can't get it in Peaslake. *Verb sap.*

C. Buy your own brewery. This is not as absurd as it sounds: the Selby Brewery, aforementioned, is tiny, almost a two-room affair. There would be worse ways for a rich man of the Freddie Laker calibre to spend his money; good beer at a decent price will always find an outlet in the clubs even if the tied-house trade is closed to it — and there could be a splendid market in Western Europe that is at the moment blanketed with keg.

CAMRA have already invested in several breweries, to obtain a shareholder's say, and are thinking of buying their own brewery, eventually. With 18,000 members it wouldn't be too difficult; after all, the Northumberland miners did just that, after 1918: the result is the brewery which you can see from the centre of Newcastle but which you can only buy in clubs, the House of Commons and the Washington Post House — THF again.

But it need not only be individuals or concerned organisations. Why not Madame Tussaud's, now thinking of making paper at Wookey Hole? Or the National Trust, if the building were a worthwhile monument and many of them are — weep for the vanished Georgian grandeur of Cobb's of Margate, disappeared under that umbrella of Whitbread's. Or indeed the DoE itself reversing the *fâcheux* — English: bloody idle — dismemberment of the state-owned Carlisle Brewery, which wore a highly acceptable face of nationalisation.

Donnington Ales brews in a Cotswold manor house. Hook Norton, ten miles away, is an astonishing steam brewery – the motive power was installed before 1900 and was second-hand then. Both are brewing splendid stuff, and may they continue for ever. But if they didn't then both buildings and brew should be recognised as a national monument and kept going on that basis.

The owners need not be national. Why shouldn't a local council own its own brewery – especially in a New Town, where it could if it wished control the outlets also? Milton Keynes, or Central Lancashire New Town; the one I am thinking about most sharply is Telford. Because Greenall Whitley of Warrington bought up the Wrekin brewery there and closed it in 1968. They still brew at Wem, north of Shrewsbury, and it is a decent pint, but it isn't the same. Only 20 miles away, but quite different – the essence of British regional difference, just like the British landscape.

Wrekin was a very light-coloured beer – like the vanished West Country Ales at Gloucester – with a penetrating flavour. You can get some idea of it in the light mild brewed by the All Nations at Madeley – one of the four home-brew pubs left in Britain: the others are at Bishop's Castle, Natherton, in the Black Country, and Helston in Cornwall. So the recipe is still there: how about it, Telford New Town, a bit of old England to match the new England of the Town Centre?

The real test will be what happens at Barnsley. The situation there has all the disparate reasons for not closing a brewery rolled into one: a splendid regional flavour – not as good as it was a couple of years ago, but that process is easily reversed; massive local support, and remarkably handsome buildings, in a wooded valley, perhaps the best architecture in Barnsley. The 1976 beer cup final looks like being CAMRA versus Courage. It should be quite a fight.

Finally, further reading, which is essential unless you already know all about brewing and all about the local brews. Three books have appeared in the last year which dovetail beautifully. Christopher Hutt's *The Death of the English Pub* (Arrow, 75p) is a splendid polemic to alert you to the danger. Frank Baillie's *Beer Drinker's Companion* (David & Charles £2.95) is more leisurely but just as tough, and gives details of all the independent brewers in Britain. *The Good Beer Guide* (CAMRA 75p) tells you where to get the real stuff, and Richard Boston stirs things up every Saturday in the *Guardian*. CAMRA lives at 94 Victoria Street, St Albans, and £1 yearly subscription will get you an admirable monthly magazine that will tell you just what is happening to beer all round the country. For the first time in decades, the news is not all bad: ladies and gents of the thirsting classes, I think we are going to win this struggle in the end.

Sunday Times, 30 June 1974

THE GOLIATH ALE

Richard Jeffries

By Flamma's side there stood a great mug of the Goliath ale, and between his lips there was a long churchwarden pipe.

The Goliath ale was his mineral water; his gaseous, alkaline, chalybeate liquor; better by far than Kissingen, Homburg, Vichy; better by far than mud baths and hot springs. There is no medicine in nature, or made by man, like good ale. He who drinks ale is strong.

The bitter principle of the aromatic hops went to his nervous system, to the much-suffering liver, to the clogged and weary organs, bracing and stimulating, urging on, vitalizing anew.

The spirit drawn from the joyous barley warmed his heart; a cordial grown on the sunny hill-side, watered with dew and sweet rain, coloured by the light, a liquor of sunshine, potable sunbeam.

Age mingling hops and barley in that just and equitable proportion, no cunning of hand, no science can achieve, gave to it the vigour of years, the full manhood of strength.

There was in it an alchemic power analysis cannot define. The chemist analyses, and he finds of ten parts, there are this and there are that, and the residue is "volatile principle", for which all the dictionaries of science have no explanation.

"Volatile principle" — there it is, that is the secret. That is the life of the thing; by no possible means can you obtain that volatile principle — that alchemic force — except contained in genuine old ale.

Only it must be genuine, and it must be old; such as Iden brewed.

The Idens had been famous for ale for generations.

By degrees Alere's hand grew less shaky; the glass ceased to chink against his teeth; the strong, good ale was setting his Fleet Street liver in order.

You have "liver", you have "dyspepsia", you have "kidneys", you have "abdominal glands", and the doctor tells you you must take bitters, i.e., quassia, buchu, gentian, cascarilla, calumba; aperients and diluents, podophyllin, taraxacum, salts; physic for the nerves and blood, quinine, iron, phosphorus; this is but the briefest outline of your draughts and preparations; add to it for various purposes, liquor arsenicalis, bromide of potassium, strychnia, belladonna.

Weary and disappointed, you turn to patent medicines — American and French patent physic is very popular now — and find the same things precisely under taking titles, enormously advertised.

It is a fact that nine out of ten of the medicines compounded are intended to produce exactly the same effects as are caused by a few glasses of good old ale. The objects are to set the great glands in motion, to regulate the stomach, brace the nerves, and act as a tonic and cordial; a little ether put in to aid the digestion of the compound. This is precisely what good old ale does, and digests itself very comfortably. Above all things, it contains the volatile principle, which the prescriptions have not got.

Many of the compounds actually are beer, bittered with quassia instead of hops; made nauseous in order that you may have faith in them.

"Throw physic to the dogs," get a cask of the true Goliath, and "drenk un down to the therd hoop."

Amaryllis at the Fair, 1887

SAVING A LEGENDARY BEER

Roger Protz

It's not my habit to sneak into pubs by the back door at 10 o'clock in the morning for an early snifter but this was – I promise, m'lud – purely in the interests of research. The previous evening I had had the first taste of Draught Burton Ale – DBA for short – brewed by the Burton Bridge Brewery for the town's CAMRA beer festival and was bewitched, overjoyed and generally knocked asunder by the beer's glorious aroma and palate. The beer came straight from the cask and the brewers at Burton Bridge, Geoff Mumford and Bruce Wilkinson, suggested I might care to compare the beer when pulled through a beer engine. It was too good a challenge to turn down and so I reported for duty the next morning at their brewery tap, the Burton Bridge Inn.

My verdict was simple: the beer was superb and I enjoyed the fact that – pulled to the bar – it had a tad more luscious hop character than the gravity version of the night before.

More importantly, the appearance of DBA in Burton was a small but not unimportant victory for both brewers' bravery and consumers' determination to save a legendary beer from the knackers' yard. On the opening night of the festival on 26 March, two nine-gallon firkins of DBA disappeared down drinkers' throats in two hours. There was an even speedier response in the Bridge Inn: two "nines" were emptied in 1½ hours. The good folk of Burton-on-Trent are proud of their beers and the town's brewing legacy.

The reason for the excitement was that DBA was declared dead and buried in January by the brand's owner, Carlsberg UK. I wrote about this decision at the time, and a brief resume will suffice. The beer – originally called Ind Coope Draught Burton Ale – was first brewed in 1976 and its success helped kick-start the real ale revival. Ind Coope, with breweries in Burton and Romford, was part of the national group Allied Breweries. Allied at the time was best known for Double Diamond keg bitter and Skol lager. Its return to cask ale reverberated throughout the industry and encouraged the other giant national brewers to return to the fold.

But the beer fell victim to the shenanigans in the brewing industry in the 1980s and 90s. Allied became Allied Lyons and then Allied Domecq. Neither Lyons nor Domecq had much interest in beer and the Allied brewing interests were sold to Carlsberg. DBA moved around the chess board to Marston's, then Tetley in Leeds and finally to J. W. Lees in Manchester. Sales, once buoyant, dwindled. The beer was available in only a handful of pubs. Unloved and unwanted by Carlsberg, the group pulled the plug.

The response was rapid. Burton's MP, Andrew Griffiths, lobbied Carlsberg to release the brand so that another brewer could produce it. At the same time, three CAMRA members in Derby, John Arguile, Dave Evans and Les Baynton, formed BLOTTS — Beer Lovers On T'Tour — with the aim of restoring such lost Burton beers as DBA. They held talks with Geoff Mumford and Bruce Wilkinson at Burton Bridge and as a result a batch of beer was brewed for the local beer festival.

Geoff Mumford and Bruce Wilkinson were the ideal people to brew the beer as they had worked for Ind Coope and helped formulate the recipe. They told me DBA was based on the bottled, 4.7%, version of Double Diamond. Mumford and Wilkinson are at pains to stress that it's not possible to recreate a beer that tastes exactly the same as the DBA of the 1970s. They are able to use similar if not identical malts and hops, along with the legendary Burton spring waters, but they don't have access to the yeast culture used by Ind Coope.

Pale and crystal malts are joined by four English hops, Challenger, Fuggles, Goldings and Target with Styrian Goldings added for "dry hopping" — hops added to each cask for additional aroma.

It has a rich malty aroma with a fine floral hop character and a fruit note reminiscent of lime marmalade. Juicy malt, lemon-and-lime fruit and floral hop resins combine on the palate, while the finish starts bittersweet but ends dry with a good hop bitterness balanced by continuing ripe malt and citrus fruit.

It's a delicious beer, and let's hope it can continue to be produced. Burton Bridge will produce 50 barrels a week while demand is high. "We'll shoe-horn it into our range," Wilkinson says, "but if it continues we'll have to take another beer out."

In the grand scheme of things, a small batch of beer on sale in 16 pubs won't change the world. But DBA is a beer that represents the history and heritage of a renowned brewing town and needs to be revered and restored. A lot will depend on the attitude of Carlsberg. Will it turn the other cheek, take legal action or agree to hand over brand names and trademarks? The company hasn't reached a decision yet, but all lovers of great Burton beers will hope for a positive outcome.

Publican's Morning Advertiser, 30 March 2015

THE MOST BITTER BEER IN BELGIUM

Breandán Kearney

In the 1990s, small breweries in Belgium were being bought up by industrial brewing conglomerates, and the market was dominated by sweet mass-produced beers. Enter the XX Bitter, a pale ale of 6.2% ABV from Brouwerij De Ranke. It would become known, for a time at least, as the most bitter beer in Belgium.

"I started home brewing at the end of the 1970s," says Nino Bacelle, Head Brewer at Brouwerij De Ranke. "I wasn't very successful then so I followed courses at a brewery school in the 1980s." Nino's father was a beer distributor and the family owned a small lemonade factory. By 1994, Nino was brewing beer commercially at Deca Services, a brewing facility in West Flanders which De Struise Brouwers use to this day. "I learned to work on old equipment," says Nino. "It was there that I found out I was making better beer than some of the bigger industrial brewers." Nino attributes the quality of De Ranke's beers to three rules. "Firstly, we use whole hops," he says. "Not extract or pellets. Secondly, we never filter our beers. And thirdly, we never pasteurise our beers."

Nino met Guido Devos and they started Brouwerij De Ranke in 1996. Guido ran a beer-tasting club at the time and together they decided to brew a test batch of beer that used a lot of hops. "That was the first test for XX Bitter," says Nino. "We put it on a festival in Kortrijk for the first time in 1996 and a lot of the brewers there told us we wouldn't be able to sell it because it was too bitter."

In 2004, they built their own brewery. "In effect, the current De Ranke brewery is a copy of the old-fashioned brewery we had been working on at Deca," says Nino. "We have computer controls now but we do everything the traditional way. We use direct fire. We re-ferment in the bottle from zero pressure. We work with whole hops."

The brewery's location is a good example of the quirky reality of Belgium's geography. "I live in Wevelgem and Guido lives in Zwevegem," says Nino. "So we both live in Flanders but the brewery is a few kilometres away in French- speaking Wallonia, just across the language border. It's located in Dottignies but the official headquarters of De Ranke are at my home address so I suppose we are a Flemish brewery."

This new De Ranke brewery has been an important breeding ground for other highly regarded Belgian breweries. Yvan De Baets worked part-time at the brewery between 2004 and 2006 before setting up Brasserie De La Senne with Bernard Leboucq. Yvan and Bernard gypsy-brewed at

De Ranke between 2006 and 2009 but De La Senne now have their own brewing facility in the Molenbeek area of Brussels. Alex Lippens and Koen Van Lancker of Brouwers Verzet also gypsy-brew at Brouwerij De Ranke. They've just bought their own system which is set to arrive in the first half of 2016. De Ranke's XX Bitter is still regarded as a trendsetter for hop forward brewing in Belgium. It may not be the most bitter beer in Belgium anymore, but it showcases hops in a way that many breweries are reluctant (or perhaps unable) to do and it demonstrates a balance in its flavours.

So what is it? Some refer to it as a golden ale. Ratings websites list it as an India Pale Ale. Belgians generally don't give much notice to style nomenclatures anyway, but how would the brewer of the beer describe XX Bitter?

"It's a bitter pale ale," says Nino. "When we first made XX Bitter, the IPA trend hadn't started yet. We didn't even know what it was. Technically it probably fits into what an IPA is, but we never had this in mind."

XX Bitter is hopped with two varieties of European hops which give the beer both a grassy, earthy quality and an IBU level of 65. "We use Brewer's Gold for bittering," says Nino. "And Hallertau Mittelfreuh for aroma. All of our hops are grown in a nearby forest farm here in Wallonia. We only use hops grown in Belgium. We have more control that way. We don't dry-hop and we only use single additions of each. By using only hop flowers, we ensure the hop oils are never oxidised so we never get any harsh bitterness in our beers." De Ranke brew the "grandmother's way", adding hot water to achieve target mashing temperatures. Their kettles have a capacity of 4,000 litres. The other specifications of the XX Bitter are relatively simple: 100% pilsner malt from Belgium and a dry Fermentis yeast pitched directly into the fermenter.

But the yeast profile of this beer wasn't always so straightforward. "In the years we were brewing XX Bitter between 1994 and 1998, we were using Rodenbach yeast," says Nino. "Because of that, the beer developed some sourness after about six months. There were Brettanomyces characteristics and some lactic acid bacteria characteristics. But when Palm Breweries bought Rodenbach, they stopped allowing the yeast to be used by smaller breweries. That's when we changed to a Fermentis dry yeast." Today De Ranke attenuate with that dry yeast to extremely high levels. "Our beers ferment out completely," says Nino. "We condition at higher temperatures than a lot of breweries, mostly at 15°C. We also allow for four weeks of conditioning after primary fermentation, which is longer than a lot of other breweries. This gives us a really dry beer."

There's also an XXX Bitter, a beer made at the request of an American beer festival. "They wanted us to make a dry-hopped version of the XX Bitter," says Nino. "But instead we added 50% more hops. If we use 10 grams of hops per litre for the XX Bitter, we use 15 grams of hops per litre for the XXX Bitter."

The trilogy of the Guldenberg (their 8% ABV/40 IBU interpretation of a Belgian *tripel*), the Saison de Dottiginies (a dry well-hopped beer of 5.5% ABV in a style typical for the region) and the Hop Harvest (an ale of 6% ABV brewed in the week of the hop harvest) showcases De Ranke's skills in brewing with hops.

But they are far from being a one-trick pony. Their Noir de Dottignies (9% ABV) is brewed with seven different malts and the amber-coloured Père Noël (7% ABV) is not your typical Christmas ale.

And then there's the sour, dry and complex Cuvée De Ranke (7% ABV), a blend of barrel-aged beer, fresh top-fermented beer and lambic from Girardin. Using a similar process they use cherries to produce a Kriek De Ranke (7% ABV). But why choose lambic from Girardin? "We think they make the best one-year old lambic," says Nino. "I'm not talking about Geuze here. Just unblended base lambic. For us, some lambics are too one-dimensional. But we really like the lambic from Girardin. "

XX Bitter remains one of their most popular beers. They brew 5,000HL of beer a year at De Ranke and 1,500HL of that is XX Bitter. 50% of their beer is exported outside Belgium, mostly to Italy and the US, but also to Japan, India, the Netherlands, the UK, Sweden, Denmark, France and Austria.

How did it get its name? "I liked the names of the English beers," says Nino. "They were called Bitter. Special Bitter. Extra Special Bitter. But they weren't very bitter. I wanted the name to be a bit like that. And I wanted it to say that this was a bitter beer."

www.belgiansmaak.com, 13 January 2016

Its Brass-Bright Depths

Dylan Thomas

I liked the taste of beer, its live, white lather, its brass-bright depths, the sudden world through the wet-brown walls of the glass, the tilted rush to the lips and the slow swallowing down to the lapping belly, the salt on the tongue, the foam at the corners.

Portrait of the Artist as a Young Dog, 1940

Mr Hackett's Demon Beers

Byron Rogers

I.

"And just look at this one." Anthony Hackett might have been handling a plague bacillus. *La Bière du Démon*. "Beer of the Demon," translated Hackett, peering through his reading glasses at the bearded face, not unlike his own, which leered out of the label. "That's 12 per cent, that is, 12 per cent alcohol." He replaced the bottle carefully among the long rows that covered the table. Screw-topped bottles, metal-topped, china-stoppered, huge green champagne-corked things, held down with what seemed to be barbed wire, deadly little brown bottles. Not one had less than 7 per cent alcohol.

"It's the lavatories that worry me," said Hackett suddenly. "Over there they're just cupboards in a corner of the bar; anyone can find his way out of a cupboard. Ours are up the garden. Half a dozen of them demons and we'd need search parties for our regulars."

This is the story of a good man, an English publican who, fearful of what 1992 might unleash on his customers, earlier this year disappeared for four months. Now there were those who maintained he had disappeared long ago, who muttered he had only been seen twice in eight years behind his own bar, but they missed the point. Like one of Arthur's knights, Mr Hackett of the Bartholomew Arms in Blakesley, near Towcester, was on a quest.

In his cabin cruiser, accompanied by his wife, Sylvia, Hackett sailed into the canal systems of Europe to bring back the beers that will change forever the old habits of Middle England. For in 1992 men should for the first time in their lives know what they are drinking. No foaming agents, no anti-oxidants. No ground fish guts, onion rings or potato peelings. In short, none of the little incidentals which bring the reassuring headache in the morning. Just this one chilling statement on label after label: "Ingredients: water, malt, hops".

Under the huge wet skies of northern France, Hackett floated on, his boat bobbing like a cork in the wash of barges carrying a thousand Renaults. And like Lancelot, he came on many marvels, beers of such quality, their sell-by date two whole years into the future. He found beers flavoured with real fruit ("7 per cent of strawberries and torrid pleasure"), beers made to medieval recipes, beers brewed by Trappist monks. "Imagine the vicar running a distillery", Hackett said.

Shady lock-keepers pressed honey on him, which he loathes, and goat's cheese, which he loathes even more, both on the unspoken premise that if he didn't buy them, the great gates might not open in his lifetime. One man got him to buy a bottle of home-made eau-de-vie. "He made me taste it. My God. My brain went out through one ear and I found I'd given him £10." Later he met a German doctor and warned him about the lock-keeper. The doctor asked for a taste. It wasn't dangerous, then? No, no, said the doctor, his eyes closed: it was the Mirabelle. But the lock-keeper made it in the woods, insisted Hackett. The best place, said the doctor.

Near Strasbourg he met a man who made him lace his beer with herbal bitters. "It was unspeakably vile. I told him it was the most wonderful thing I had ever tasted," said Hackett the European. In High Germany, his boat low in the water and clinking audibly, he had his portrait painted and sent home so his customers might not forget him or what he was up to on their behalf.

The portrait shows a youthful Hackett, the years fallen

away, his beard curling like that of a Norse god. But in Blakesley the customers had an art teacher at a local school produce a replica, using the same crayons, the same coloured paper, the same frame. Only this time there were great bags under the eyes and the mouth was twisted into a sneer. When Ulysses returned to Ithaca, this thing faced him in his own bar. "My God!" said Ulysses. "Those four months must have aged me."

But he had his revenge.

2.

The most momentous thing that can happen to a pub, short of closure, is a change of brew. Regulars see no reason to change their ways, so when, as happened locally in the Royal Oak at Eydon, the Watney's is taken out and replaced by Everard's Old Original, they find themselves walking politely into walls. So it was that finally, at the Bartholomew Arms, Mr Hackett held a tasting to prepare his customers for what the European Union might unleash upon them.

There were five of us: Mr Blake, a driver; Mr Vaughan, an advertising man; Mr Matthews, a marketing manager; Mr Penney, a company director; and me — late twentieth-century yokels all. I had not met Mr Penney before. "Shirts," he said.

"Ah," I said. Two years ago at the local fête I acquired four of his brand new shirts at 25p each, his wife having given them without his knowledge. "They're wearing well," I said brightly.

"Good," he said.

Now, when they held beer tastings on the *Food and Drink* programme, Mr Oz Clarke talked dreamily about the scents of summer and that excitable blonde went pop-eyed with joy.

But then they only had five bottles, and sipped. We had 50 and did not sip.

"Jam," sneered Mr Blake.

Looking back, it was a mistake to start with the Belgian fruit beers. There was poor staff work (none of us could translate *framboise*), followed by incredulity at the taste and smell. But there was a beachhead and we moved on. To Chimay. A Belgian beer, made by Trappist monks vowed equally to silence and brewing. How we laughed at this — until we drank it.

"Have you got the fire on or is it just me?" asked Mr Matthews, taking off his sweater. After Chimay, spectacles made an appearance and all the labels were read. Chimay is 8 per cent alcohol.

"Barley Wine," muttered Mr Blake. "Just Barley Wine and Honey."

There was open country for a while and we moved easily among the light little lagers of France. "Too weak," said Mr Blake. Then the advance ground to a halt and there was much reconnaissance of Brigand, a Belgian beer. How much? Nine per cent. Good God! Like the veterans we were becoming, we settled into our trenches and waited for it to do its worst. At this point there was a long discussion on the strategy of the Gulf War, during which Mr Hackett, an old submariner, said it was up to the Navy. But it was a desert war, ventured someone, for they were his beers after all. Element of surprise, boomed Mr Hackett.

"Shouldn't touch that Brigand with a bargepole," said Mr Matthews.

"You not only touched it, you've just drunk it."

"Oh yes," said Mr Matthews.

Some of the time we knew where we were. There was even a familiar brew, Kronenbourg 1664. "Look, only 5.9 per cent," said Mr Matthews, which was an indication of how far we had come. Another indication was Mr Hackett handing Mr Matthews a screw-top bottle to open, and, at the same time, handing him a corkscrew. But we had learned to treat a dark colour and a smell of toffee with respect. It was just that occasionally there was a ringer. *Bière du Désert*, read out a linguist. "That means Desert Beer." It was excellent, not sweet, and led you unsuspectingly into the desert. How much? Seven per cent. It isn't. It is. French? Yes. Typical of them to make a sneaky beer like that. So we drank Eku, an honest German brew that was exactly what it said it was: "The Strongest Beer in the World" — 11 per cent.

"Can someone get me a bitter?" appealed Mr Blake. "I need to remember what beer tastes like."

There were lagers and beers dancing with sediment, which, on account of the language problem, we had shaken up. We did not drink them all, adopting the American naval strategy in the Pacific of allowing some to surrender in their own time. "Just look at their shelf life," marvelled Mr Hackett.

The lives we had led until this were elsewhere, so that Mr Matthews did not even bring up the subject of his recent circumcision until well after midnight. And then only in the one-act, condensed version. I walked quietly home with Mr Blake up half-known roads. There is a village in England now where men fear Europe.

1998

2

BEER IN PUBS

Two inches to the north-west is written a word
full of meaning – the most purposeful word that
can be written on a map. Inn.

A.A. Milne

REBUS ON DRAUGHT

Ian Rankin

A pub is a great place for a writer to be. They have always been fascinating social laboratories where you get a mix of people from different backgrounds, different jobs, different attitudes — just like on *Big Brother*. Every pub is *Big Brother* writ large.

Beer is a great equaliser because it's not an expensive product, it's what people tend to drink at the end of a hard day. Because it's quite cheap, it's egalitarian.

When I first went to the Oxford Bar in the 1980s, I was struck by this great mix of students and lawyers, police officers and mechanics, the unemployed, the disenfranchised, the political, the apolitical, the upper classes, the lower classes. It was a wonderful melting-pot.

That's also what makes a pub a great place for a cop. If a detective wants to find out how a city works, a pub is the place to go. You'll overhear stories, you'll be told stories. And, at the end of your working day, where else are you going to let off steam? The vast majority of us let off steam in the pub.

A pub is also a kind of community. The regulars who drink with Rebus in the Oxford Bar are as close to a family as he's got. Ironically, sometimes these are people whose surnames he doesn't know, and he doesn't know what they do for a living. But for an hour, or a couple of hours, they know each other and they relax.

Pubs are the measure of community in modern Britain. You see that in the soap operas. The two most successful soaps in the UK - *EastEnders* and *Coronation Street* - both revolve around a pub, and there's a good reason for that. Pubs localise things. The "local" is where the people from that city or town or village discuss the issues that are relevant to them.

I think Rebus likes the fact that in a pub you can strike up a conversation with a complete stranger, you don't have to give too much of yourself away. It's a refuge from the real world, but at the same time, you can find out quite a lot about the real world in a good pub.

When he meets an informant in a pub, he's carrying on a grand old Scottish and Edinburgh tradition which is using the pub as your place of work. There was a time in Edinburgh's history when, if you wanted to see a lawyer, you went to a pub. The lawyer didn't have an office, he had a certain place in a pub where he would sit and work and clients would come in and meet him. It's a grand old tradition, and one writers keep up to this day.

I find pubs a great source of ideas. Beermats are a godsend to me. Often I come home from a night in the pub with five or six beermats in my pocket, all with ideas written down on them: jokes, characters, one-liners, things that people have said. Right from the start of the Rebus series, from about the fourth page of the first book, you're in a pub.

Some of the best times I've ever had in my life have been in pubs. My wife Miranda and I cemented our relationship in a pub. We were at university together, and we went to the same lectures and tutorials, but it was afterwards in the pub that the big ideas got talked about. In a tutorial you were too embarrassed to speak in case you got it wrong, but in the pub you had the freedom to spark off different ideas. There were no right or wrong answers in the pub.

Beer has always been part of the experience of living in Edinburgh. It's strange to stand in the Caledonian Brewery and realise that it is the only working brewery left in the city, when there used to be more than 40. The Scottish Parliament sits on the site of a brewery.

When I came here as a student, one of the things you were

aware of was the smell of hops. You couldn't escape it. If you were walking along early in the morning or late at night, you would always smell that smell. It permeates the books.

A lot of the major buildings in the city, such as the Usher Hall and the McEwan Hall, were named after brewing dynasties. These were the people who made the money and they ploughed it back into creating buildings like concert halls. Now, I think the resonances are in danger of being lost. People don't realise the connection because you can't get a pint of Usher's any more.

I'm not saying all pubs are good, and you shouldn't sit in pubs all day to the detriment of other parts of your existence, but a good pub is a godsend. It can be your entertainment centre, your psychiatrist. If you're down, people ask you what's wrong with you. The Scots are quite reticent as a race, we don't easily spill our troubles to strangers, but there's something about a pub that means you can do that, and you're not going to be judged. There's nothing judgemental about a good pub.

Good pubs are in danger. There's a trend in the industry towards uniformity, and to me a good pub is something unique. If you walk into a place and it looks the same as another pub, it has the same music system playing the same songs and you get the same beer, it can be a little deflating.

What you want from a good pub is character. And these are the days of superpubs, huge ghettos piling people in for half-price drinks. To me that's not a pub, that's a meat market. A good pub is somewhere fairly quiet where you can enjoy a good conversation, and it should be a manageable size for the people who use it, not a vast aircraft hangar with a few loudspeakers.

We have a terrible reputation in Scotland for hard drinking, for not drinking responsibly. But a good pub doesn't keep forcing drink down your throat. A good pub is where the barman will say: "Ian, you've had enough," and phone you a taxi.

And the drinking culture in Scotland is changing. It has changed seismically even in the time since I started drinking. We don't just drink to get drunk any more, there's a much more social element to it. These days, we don't feel we need to go completely over the edge, to defining ourselves by how much we can drink. You don't prove yourself a hardman by drinking yourself into oblivion, almost the opposite.

The nature of the pub has changed, and I think it's changed for the better. They're more welcoming. The old cliché of the kids sitting outside on the doorstep eating crisps while their parents are inside just doesn't work any more.

The smoking ban has been wonderful for Scotland. Our bars are going to become more like continental bars; they won't just offer booze, they'll offer soft drinks, hot drinks, all sorts of things. The Oxford Bar, God bless them, have installed a coffee machine, so now you can have a cappuccino. I've never seen anybody have one, but the coffee machine is there.

Rebus isn't going to like the smoking ban, but he's going to have to deal with it. I know guys who smoke more than him and they've had to deal with it. In the next book, he's going to be stepping outside to have his cigarette.

I've been drinking in the Oxford Bar since 1984, since I was a postgraduate student and my flatmate was the part-time barman. And yet the place hasn't changed. It's changed ownership several times, but physically it hasn't changed. It's like a TARDIS. It's got a life of its own, a mind of its own, and it's bigger on the inside than it is on the outside.

It makes no difference to anyone there that my books have become bestsellers. It would be terrible if it did. It would take more than that to make a difference to anybody that drinks in the Oxford Bar. The minute you walk over the threshold, there's a democracy at work. As long as you've got money in your pocket for a drink, you're the same as everybody else.

The Lord Provost could be in there, or a politician, a senior lawyer, a football star, and if they ever try to get above themselves they'll very quickly find out that's not going to work. Every punter in there is the same. The guy who delivers the post, the guy who works at Waverley Station, has exactly the same stature as any musician or writer or rock star who happens to walk in. I love that.

Scotsman, 27 January 2007

IT WAS GOING TO BE A LONG NIGHT AT U FLEKŮ . . .

Adrian Tierney-Jones

I had parked myself at the end of a long wooden table, lights reflected on its well-tanned surface like a crooked selection of smiles. It was a mighty, majestic table, and as well as bearing witness to the buff brush of thousands of elbows it was pock-marked with all the warts and wattles of age, as were its fellow travellers in the room. For a brief *Lord of the Rings* moment I thought it carved out of a single tree — but an inner voice whispered (with the treacherous hiss of a latter-day Gollum, perhaps) that its real maternal home might actually be a ware-house (and associated website) whose owner had made their name in supplying Czech pubs such as U Fleků with suitably Gothic adornments.

Meanwhile the bench that the table held dominion over seemed pulled straight from the suffer-the-little-children school of canes, cold baths and compulsory Latin. And yet in spite of the forbidding and elemental appearance of sternness, the furniture was surprisingly comfortable in the chiselled, gravel-voiced, Valhalla-lite ambience of this central European beer-hall.

The table belonged to a family of eight that I counted laid out barrack-square tidy against the wooden panels that reached halfway up the wall on both sides of the room; the pub had eight similarly furnished rooms into which tourists were funnelled as soon as they crossed the threshold from the street outside. If you've never been to Prague and know nothing about the city, or if you have but shown no interest in its beery heritage, then imagine a place like U Flekůas a beery totem pole standing at the centre of the city's tourist industry, a station of the cross at which disciples pause and pray, or maybe a place from where the call from the muezzin conjoins the faithful to the evening's reflection. It is on the map, part of the plan for a Prague stroll, a go-to place and in the top 20 hits that revolve around Prague. I think you might get the idea.

My visit to U Fleků had not been planned when I emerged from the smooth confines of the metro, wary and weary, but eager to catch a wave on the swell of people tramping through the late afternoon September sunshine. I walked amongst them, but not of them, through the canyon-tall streets, gazing upwards at Prague's fabulous architectural pick and mix of baroque, Art Nouveau, Renaissance, Gothic and French Imperial styles. A quicksilver decision, a look at a map; there was time enough to take myself off to U Fleků, before an appointment with a brewer at another brewpub (U Medvídků if you must know).

Carrying on, I had stopped again and looked at my map. A man in a bobble hat, thick coat incongruous in the sunshine, a face like a scrawl on a wall, asked me if he could help. I replied that I was OK, a bit sharply perhaps, suspicious, perhaps, as is my way (years ago I learnt while travelling to reply to anyone

I felt might be undesirable in Welsh — that soon had me left alone). No offence taken, it seemed, he then asked, "Do you want to buy some Krona?" I smiled, said no thanks, flapping my hand in front of me, and carried on, puzzled by the sort of exchange I thought had gone out of fashion when the Cold War had toppled off the catwalk of history accompanied by the mood music of a disjointed model's fall.

I thought briefly of him as I took my table and wondered what his life was like. A rapid flurry of images of decline fed some inner conveyor belt before I returned to the now and nodded to the couple on the adjoining table, against which I had squeezed, rucksack clamped to my torso with the familiarity of a firm handshake, aware of the ripples of sweat rolling down my back. They were holding hands across the salt and pepper and for a brief moment I thought they looked aggrieved to have a neighbour. I was sweaty, unshaven and wearing worn (but comfortable) climbing boots, dark blue cargo trousers and a combat jacket out of whose numerous pockets poked a variety of pens, notebooks and maps.

Settled in my chair, table flat in front of me like the Hungarian plains across which the invaders of Europe progressed century after century, I opened my notepad and started to write, to record my thoughts on what I saw and felt.

"Are you a writer?" asked the man on the next table, ignoring his companion who looked at me with a certain sense of irritation. He spoke uncertain English with a brisk German inflection. He'd probably noted the tiny Union Jack stitched onto the arm of my jacket, a heraldic reminder of its secondhand surplus nature.

"Journalist," I corrected him kindly. "Yes, also a writer. I've wanted to visit this place for a long time, taste the beer. It's good, I'm told — I write about beer.'

"The beer," he said, "is not bad for Czech beer, but we have good beer in Germany. Perhaps better." He paused. "Write about beer? You must have the best job in the world."

I nodded and smiled, but really wanted to tell him to see my tax returns. Writing about beer isn't the most lucrative career in the world, but on the other hand . . . He lifted his glass of beer to me in salute and returned to his companion, who gave me a brief tight smile of cold politeness.

The room in which I sat, within the company of a smattering of drinkers, no doubt tourists like myself and my neighbours, unveiled itself to me as a Teutonic-like shrine to dark wood, though September's late afternoon sunlight softened the hardness as it reached in and stroked the stained glass windows. I noted the large metal chandeliers that swooped down from the ceiling, cold, cruel-eyed predators dressed up as a nice interior design feature whose creator perhaps hoped for a touch of the *Nibelungenlied*. Sadly, they really looked like they'd emerged from a job lot in an out-of-town DIY store whose wares were bedded down on an industrial estate. Perhaps it was the same place from where the tables were torn from their womb.

As I waited to be served by waiters who rushed about, their trays held high, leathery, battered money bags hanging like ancient sporrans on their aprons, I continued to look: the floors were tiled, sounding-boards against which clicked the waiters' heels.

The men, and yes, they were all men as far as I could see, were typically European (no New World have-a-nice-day schmoozing here) in their froideur, imperious and the very opposite of idle in the rush with which they scurried about, holding trays studded with glasses of the rich dark lager brewed somewhere else within the building. Somewhere in the building, somewhere near and yet far, somewhere this beer that I hadn't tried was brewed within the building.

I tried to catch one's eye.

A chap of medium height stalking the next row of tables, looking about, CCTV on two legs, short stubbly hair, cropped almost to the scalp, saw me. He reached the end of the row, turned left and approached. I was reminded of the waiters in the Alt beer-halls of Düsseldorf — hard-faced, attitudinal, fast movers, forever hunting for customers, with the glacial calmness of supermodels, leaving you gratified that they haven't been rude. I presume they worked on being paid for every beer sold. The law of the jungle, Darwinian, brought to the pub. No matter. At last I was going to try a beer that had haunted me ever since reading about it within the pages of Michael Jackson's books on beer. This was my fourth visit to the city, and with a bit of time and being on my own for once, cut off from the usual press pack I normally turned up with, I was not to be denied.

As I anticipated my beer the evening's entertainment began: a scowling, mustachioed accordionist stood in the doorway and started to play the melody from "Que Sera Sera". As his fingers jabbed away with a mesmeric fluidity, the newsreel that still existed in one part of my brain uncovered an image of Doris Day singing the same song in some film from the 1950s. It was a surreal memory that I shook away with the natural ease of a large dog shuddering itself after emerging from a dip in the river.

Dressed in Rupert Bear-style checked trousers and wearing a cap of indeterminate shape, it seemed to me that the accordionist had the air of a 19th century Corsican bandit, albeit with a general comical air of buffoonish villainy. He was meant for a bad opera.

The beer arrived. It was creamy and dark with satisfying notes of liquorice and mocha coffee, all held together with a sparkling condition that gave it a beautiful drinkability along with a deft dab of bitterness in the finish. As I let the beer transport me into a different state of reverie, the man with the air of a 19th century Corsican bandit finished his song, slung his accordion on his shoulder like it was the sort of bag that usually held shot pigeons and other game, and began to root through his pocket. He brought out what I presumed was loose change and looked at it in a meaningful way, occasionally glancing up at the drinkers in the room.

Was this a big hint that the meagre audience should be lobbing money his way? As the waiters continued to roam up and down poking menu cards in the air, possibly in the hope of summoning diners out of nowhere, while flourishing silver trays of the local liqueur for more victims, I thought that for them and the snarling accordionist it was going to be a long night. Time to leave. I was due at U Medvídků very shortly, but more importantly I had an early start in the morning.

I finished my glass and covered it with a beer mat (as one does in places like this) and beckoned a waiter. I wanted to pay and leave. The drinking culture of this part of the world is replete with all manner of symbols and behavioural tics: for instance, in 19th century Prague, as Peter Demetz wrote in *Prague in Black and Gold*, "Waitresses made a little cross on the wooden top of the mug, the assumption being that nobody would be satisfied with one beer alone and that it would be difficult later to account for the many consumed (the custom has endured: present-day waiters make pencil marks on the round cardboard coasters for the beer glasses)." So that was why I covered my beer with a beer mat. I didn't want any more. I had been to U Fleků, and it was doubtful I would return on my own again.

www.maltworms.co.uk, June 2015

THE MARQUIS OF GRANBY

Charles Dickens

The Marquis of Granby, in Mrs Weller's time, was quite a model of a roadside public-house of the better class — just large enough to be convenient, and small enough to be snug. On the opposite side of the road was a large sign-board on a high post, representing the head and shoulders of a gentleman with an apoplectic countenance, in a red coat with deep blue facings, and a touch of the same blue over his three-cornered hat, for a sky. Over that again were a pair of flags; beneath the last button of his coat were a couple of cannon; and the whole formed an expressive and undoubted likeness of the Marquis of Granby of glorious memory.

The bar window displayed a choice collection of geranium plants, and a well-dusted row of spirit phials. The open shutters bore a variety of golden inscriptions, eulogistic of good beds and neat wines; and the choice group of countrymen and hostlers lounging about the stable door and horse-trough, afforded presumptive proof of the excellent quality of the ale and spirits which were sold within. Sam Weller paused, when he dismounted from the coach, to note all these little indications of a thriving business, with the eye of an experienced traveller; and having done so, stepped in at once, highly satisfied with everything he had observed.

The Pickwick Papers, 1836

SHOULD WE CHANGE THE SIGN?

We recently acquired a public house with an extremely bad reputation; the mention of the name is sufficient to condemn it with the inhabitants of the town. Our object is to remedy this, and it occurred to us that a change of sign might be advantageous. Is there any reason why we should not alter name, also do we require any permission? What is the procedure?

You do not say in your query how the poor reputation of purchased house developed. And good name in such a case depends as a rule not only upon the personality of tenants, but the character of produce retailed, and not a little upon the status of regular and occasional customers. The sign enables the inhabitants to identify the establishment, and they may have become entirely prejudiced, and we doubt whether the mere alteration of sign board will do much good. You may be driven indeed to re-fit and re-embellish the house, place new tenants in the establishment, and supply a new type of produce over counter — a chilled and filtered beer, for instance, raised by gas pressure. As for the sign board, this can easily be altered, although it might be well to notify the Excise Authorities and Licensing Clerk of local Licensing Bench of your intention. It is very easy for a licensed house to get a bad name, and we are convinced that a very comprehensive policy will have to be adopted in order to remove the slur.

Brewers Journal, 15 February 1914

BECKY'S DIVE BAR

Boak & Bailey

In the 1960s and 1970s, you took good beer where you could get it, and if that meant descending a rickety staircase into a dingy basement with pungent-smelling toilets, so be it.

We were tipped off to the existence of Becky's Dive Bar by beer writer Des de Moor, who thought it might be a candidate for one of the first "real ale pubs" or "beer exhibitions" — somewhere whose main selling point was the availability of varied cask ales from far-flung, out-of-town breweries. In his 1976 book *Beer and Skittles*, Richard Boston supports that view, arguing that Becky "made [the Dive] a living gallery of beer from all over England, more than 10 years before anyone else did anything similar".

"Becky" was born Rebecca Mary Dunne in 1907, possibly in Dublin, though she claimed to be from "a family of Manchester coopers". She married William Willeter, a sixty-five year old widower, veteran of World War I, and experienced pub landlord, in Surrey in 1943. William's grandson, Robert, told us something of the family drama that accompanied her arrival: his grandfather and father, also Robert Charles Willeter, had been running the Golden Lion pub in Caterham, Surrey, but when Becky arrived she "took over", dividing the father and son team. Reading between the lines, the family saw her as something of a gold-digger.

Early in 1954, without Robert, they moved to 24 Southwark Street, London SE1, in the basement of the Hop Exchange. The Exchange is a vast, grandly Victorian building occupying an entire block, and one which any passing beer geek will certainly have noticed: it is decorated all over with hops and hop bines. It was opened in 1867, operating, as the name suggests, as a marketplace for dealers in Kentish hops, but its builders over-estimated demand for a central hop-dealing centre, and it was never as busy as they'd hoped. Over the next eighty years or so, it was damaged by fires and bombs, partly demolished, and eventually, all but abandoned by the hop trade, its spaces were rented out as offices and shops.

According to Richard Boston, the basement premises was a sandwich shop when the Willeters took it over, though The Dive is an odd name for such a business, and it had been called that since at least 1949. Martin Green and Tony White describe it as "originally a kind of private licensed canteen for the hop merchants", which might make sense.

Unfortunately, shortly after they moved, in April 1954, William died. Thereafter, the widowed Becky appears for the first time under her own name in the London phone book as R.M. Willeter, proprietress of The Dive, with the apt phone number HOP 2335.

By the 1960s, the Dive was known as a pub specialising in serving hard-to-find out-of-town ales from casks mounted on the bar and had somehow acquired a reputation as "the oldest Free House in London" – nonsense, surely, but a telling mistake, suggesting that the place quickly came to feel like an institution. It was probably Becky who promoted this story, and she certainly put on a show for Brian Schwartz who visited in 1974 prior to writing an article for *Off Duty*, a magazine for US servicemen in Europe, rattling a set of manacles she claimed to have found in the basement, and telling stories of the Dive's various ghosts.

Ruddles, a brand now owned by Greene King, was a particular draw, as "Rutland Lives" graffito in a photo attested, but Becky was proud to say she could offer 250 different beers, including European imports from, amongst other countries, Czechoslovakia. Was she also the first publican to sell Urquell or Budvar in the UK? The pub also offered beer from Thwaites, Adnams, Duttons and Shepherd Neame at a time when those were as rare in London as today are products from, say, Mikkeller. The beer was not always good, though, at least according to CAMRA-founder Michael Hardman: "It was bloody awful, like porridge."

Recollections of Becky herself suggest a woman who, having reached her prime in the nineteen-thirties and forties, resolved to remain there. Her hair was dyed black, she wore lipstick "half an inch round her mouth", and tended to wear clothes recalling fashions of decades before, with a beehive hairdo. Maximus Bibendus recalls her having the nickname "California Becky", but no-one seems to know why.

The bar had a 78 rpm gramophone record player, which she would use to blast out songs by George Formby, Flanagan and Allen, and even the speeches of Winston Churchill, evoking the Blitz spirit in what you might call her underground shelter, when there wasn't someone playing the piano or Hammond Organ in the corner.

Those who frequented the Dive recall that she drank constantly and heavily, rarely making much sense by the end of the night, though her authority was never questioned. She was accompanied by a drunken pianist called Norman; various eccentric, heavy-drinking regulars; and a barman called Harry whose beer belly was legendary.

A blog post by Andrew Keogh — one of the few mentions of Becky's anywhere online — recalls the atmosphere and layout of the Dive Bar in the mid-seventies. It paints a picture of a dirty, scruffy, smelly pit with barely functional toilets. That view is supported by the recollections of others: "The furniture was mostly beaten-up sofas which had probably been found on a rubbish dump. A visit to the toilets was extremely hazardous as it was down the cellar steps, which were very steep and had no handrails. From memory one could have a piss and look at the casks at the same time (this was recalled by an anonymous contact called London Drinker)".

It was carpeted, too, with leftovers, scraps and "ends of rolls". It stank of urine and stale beer. Michael Hardman recalls his wife being served a gin and tonic with a fly swimming in it. When he complained, Becky speared the fly with a cocktail stick and handed the drink back.

But the Dive's foulness, decrepitude and air of eccentricity, along with the "exotic" beer, seem to have contributed to a certain cult appeal (". . . the place rocked") and an air of naughtiness.

"In the early seventies," recalls London Drinker, "I was courting a girl who worked in the same building as me in Finsbury Square. We used to trot over London Bridge regularly to Becky's as it was a place we were confident none of our respective work colleagues would find us. The attraction for us other than privacy was it sold my favourite beer of the time, Ruddles County, and my girlfriend just loved the bottled Ruddles Barley Wine."

Friday and Saturday nights, according to Andrew Keogh, were particularly hectic and exciting, and things only got busier after 1974 when the Dive was a finalist in the *Evening Standard* pub of the year award. When another small Southwark drinking establishment with cult appeal, the Rake, was named *Time Out* pub of the year in 2007, it was all but overwhelmed by new visitors for some months afterwards, and the effect of the *Standard* coverage on the Dive must have been similar.

Unfortunately, as the Dive went mainstream, its borderline-dangerous architectural features and unsanitary facilities came to the attention of the authorities. Becky cooked sausages and made sandwiches which "must have caused most of the custom at Guy's A&E on Saturday nights" in a filthy kitchen coated in grease, and it was probably this which tipped the balance. In 1975, it was forcibly closed down, and Becky, it seems, retired.

After 1975, the phone books show an R.M. Willeter moving from one place to another in London and its suburbs before eventually leaving the city behind and, via a long stint in Southend-on-Sea in Essex, ending up in Suffolk, where she died in 1997. That's right – she reached ninety years old after working for twenty years in a dangerous, unsanitary basement, with a drink constantly in her hand. Make of that what you will.

Pending further research, we can't be 100% sure what happened to the Dive next, but, by 1985, according to the CAMRA *Good Beer Guide 1986*, it was trading under the name Barker's Dive Bar, "Original floor and character all its own". Nick Boley recalls drinking there up until possibly as late as 1982 and, though Becky was gone, says the bar was still known by her name. We're not even certain which particular cellar it occupied, as both Katzenjammers and the "new" Wheatsheaf share a postal address and have similar-looking entranceways. The cellar, which is now the relocated Wheatsheaf, was, from the early nineties, a wine bar called the Hop Cellars. If that's the one, then we've got a story of the UK pub trade in microcosm: from free house to wine bar to chain pub, in the course of thirty years.

The good news for British beer drinkers was that, even as Becky's was on its last legs in the mid-seventies, real ale was making a slow comeback elsewhere and other pubs soon appeared to fill the gap in the market left by the Dive – on the beer front, at least, if not in terms of the romantic, underground dinginess and constant partying that gave it such cult appeal.

www.boakandbailey.com, July 2012

THIS CAVE OF REFRESHMENT

Patrick Hamilton

They went past the Post Office and ABC and then turned down a narrow road on their right which led indirectly towards the Cromwell Road.

Half-way down this they came to a small pub into which George led him. They got beer at the counter, and then sat at a table covered with linoleum near the door.

The long, warm, bright days still persisted, and the door of the pub was flung and fastened back. It was cool, dark, and restful inside and pleasant with the peaceful beginnings of the little house's evening trade — two men talking quietly, another reading a newspaper, the flutter of a canary in a cage, the barmaid vanishing into the other bars and returning, the occasional oily jab of the beer-engine and the soft spurt of beer. It was good to sit back in this cave of refreshment, and stare at the blinding brilliance of the day outside, the pavement, the dusty feet of temperate but jaded pedestrians.

"This is one of my regular places," said George.

"Oh yes? . . ." said Johnnie. "Very nice."

Hangover Square, 1941

ROADHOUSE AND BAR PARLOUR

John Moore

In Elmbury itself there were 28 pubs to serve a population of less than 5,000. Of course on market days this population was swelled enormously by people coming in from the country, and in the summer there were "outings and visitors from the cities as well". On the other hand, there must have been among Elmbury's 5,000, if no teetotallers at least 2,500 women, children, and sick people who drank rarely or not at all. That leaves one hundred persons to a pub. I don't understand the economics of the business, but I confess that if I wanted to be a rich man I should think twice before I took a pub in Elmbury.

The Nonconformist Ministers and the few militant teetotallers who troubled us and wrote letters to the local paper regretting "the drinking habits of Elmbury's population" always made this point about the great number of pubs in proportion to the inhabitants, and seemed to think it was a very lamentable state of affairs. But this was a great nonsense. A man doesn't drink ten drinks because there are ten pubs in his street; and if he is in the habit of drinking ten drinks he usually drinks them all in one pub. In fact, almost every man has his own "local" where the beer, the company, the darts, the landlord or the barmaid happen to be to his taste; and since men are conservative in their habits he rarely makes a change.

However, at every session of the Licensing Justices there was much talk of "redundant" licences; and from time to time they would refuse to renew the licence of some small pub, and some poor man's "local" ceased to exist. The brewers who owned most of the pubs were partly to blame for this. They were only too glad to exchange two old licences — perhaps of pleasant but unprofitable little pubs — for one new licence, promising to build a roadhouse "with large commodious bars and every modern amenity". The Justices, and oddly enough especially the teetotal justices, seemed to believe that there was some special virtue in large and commodious bars, catering for people who came in cars and charabancs, and some special wickedness in small cosy bars where old friends got together for their evening drink. But for my part I always regretted the passing of the little pubs. I'd rather sit round the fire with half a dozen good fellows in the Wheatsheaf or the Barrel and drink beer from the wood than perch myself on a high stool at a long bar in a roadhouse and be served by refained and supercilious young women with stuff called beer which comes sizzling out of a tap after having been pumped through miles of chromium-plated pipes by hundreds of pounds' worth of machinery. Nor is this just my old-fashioned obscurantism; the majority of the population, it seems, likes the little pubs also, and people from the cities drive 20 miles on Sunday morning to crowd us out of our local because they hate the roadhouses too. A pub, after all, is not just a place for convenient drinking; if it were, these modern places with their ceaseless fountains of beer would serve the purpose very well. But a pub is primarily a meeting-place for friends; where friends as well as drinking may talk, argue, play games, or just sit and think according their mood. The personal relationship with the landlord is important too; it is good that there should be a "host", for thus good manners are observed. I would rather that my host was the landlord of a little pub, a poor man drinking with his fellows, than a "manager" who has more in common with his customers than the manager of a chain-store; which is exactly what he is.

A Portrait of Elmbury, 1945

RASKOLNIKOV CLEARS HIS HEAD

Fyodr Dostoyevsky

Without stopping to think, Raskolnikov went down the steps at once. Till that moment he had never been into a tavern, but now he felt giddy and was tormented by a burning thirst. He longed for a drink of cold beer, and attributed his sudden weakness to the want of food. He sat down at a sticky little table in a dark and dirty corner; ordered some beer, and eagerly drank off the first glassful. At once he felt easier; and his thoughts became clear.

Crime and Punishment, 1866

THE LAST OF ENGLAND

Hilaire Belloc

From the towns all Inns have been driven: from the villages most . . . Change your hearts or you will lose your Inns and you will deserve to have lost them. But when you have lost your Inns drown your empty selves, for you will have lost the last of England.

This and That and the Other, 1912

THE OTHER SIDE OF THE BAR – BITTER

Matthew Curtis

A customer approaches the busy bar and spends several seconds scanning the row of pump clips in front of him. He then looks past the bar and through me as he stares at the blackboard to my left and continues to deliberate over the list of cask beers we have on draught at this moment. Eventually his focus returns to the pump clips for an instant, before eventually turning to me.

"Do you have something nice and smooth?" he asks, and as I greet him and attempt to strike up a dialogue my right hand reaches below the bar where I collect two small glasses. I hand him a taster of Five Points Pale Ale and Moor So'Hop — two of our most popular cask ales, which had been flying out that day. Both could be described as being "pale and hoppy". He sips the first and winces. "No that's too fruity," he says of the Five Points, before sipping the So'Hop and producing a similar reaction. "Don't you have something a bit more malty — a nice bitter, perhaps?"

Disaster. I had just pulled through our last pint of Stroud's excellent Tom Long Bitter, and my colleague Mars had already disappeared into the cellar to begin the process of cleaning the line and changing the barrel. It would be at least half an hour before we replaced it with our house bitter from Uley Brewery. Both satisfying and refreshing in the same instant, with a kind of golden-syrup-meets-barley-sugar sweetness in the finish — it ticks all the boxes for those who like to drink "something nice and smooth".

I decide to have one more stab at appeasing my customer and pour him a sample of Hammerton's N7 pale ale. It's perhaps even more bitter and flavourful than the two beers I'd already offered, but it's also darker in colour — more like a traditional bitter. I hoped that the pleasing amber hue would help my customer make up his mind.

"I suppose that'll do," he says, and I pull through a pint for him. He then takes up residence at the bar with a friend, who is already halfway through his second pint of our most popular keg pale ale, Beavertown Gamma Ray. He takes one sniff of his friend's pint and pulls a face that resembles a scrunched-up brown paper bag. "I don't know how you can drink that," he says, as he tucks into his equally bitter and citrusy beer with abandon.

"Is the Uley on yet?" he asks every ten minutes, gesturing towards my colleague, who is currently pulling water through the line. Not yet, I say, and so he has another half of Hammerton. A few minutes later, Mars attaches the new pump clip to the handle and begins to write up the beers information in chalk on the board behind us. Noticing the customer is midway through his half I decide to pour the pint there and then before handing it over the bar without saying a word, just giving a knowing smile.

"That's more like it," he says, taking a deep gulp from the glass. "I think I'll stay here a little longer."

www.totalales.co.uk, April 2016

THE MOON UNDER WATER

George Orwell

My favourite public-house, the Moon Under Water, is only two minutes from a bus stop, but it is on a side-street, and drunks and rowdies never seem to find their way there, even on Saturday nights.

Its clientele, though fairly large, consists mostly of "regulars" who occupy the same chair every evening and go there for conversation as much as for the beer.

If you are asked why you favour a particular public-house, it would seem natural to put the beer first, but the thing that most appeals to me about the Moon Under Water is what people call its "atmosphere".

To begin with, its whole architecture and fittings are uncompromisingly Victorian. It has no glass-topped tables or other modern miseries, and, on the other hand, no sham roof-beams, ingle-nooks or plastic panels masquerading as oak. The grained woodwork, the ornamental mirrors behind the bar, the cast-iron fireplaces, the florid ceiling stained dark yellow by tobacco-smoke, the stuffed bull's head over the mantelpiece — everything has the solid, comfortable ugliness of the nineteenth century.

In winter there is generally a good fire burning in at least two of the bars, and the Victorian lay-out of the place gives one plenty of elbow-room. There are a public bar, a saloon bar, a ladies' bar, a bottle-and-jug for those who are too bashful to buy their supper beer publicly, and, upstairs, a dining-room.

Games are only played in the public, so that in the other bars you can walk about without constantly ducking to avoid flying darts.

from "The Moon Under Water", *Evening Standard*, February 1946

No Village Should Be Without One

Ian Nairn

It may seem perverse to write about country pubs in my Pimlico locale, with Victoria Station just across the road and inner ring road traffic thundering by. But Pimlico, if not country, is still a village, and it has the same pressures as a beauty spot — hordes of tourists, plus a mass of commuters. And yet it stays intact.

How? And why is it that only England and Germany, in my experience, have real country pubs, not transplanted urban bars? Good beer, for one thing. There are parts of Bavaria where every other village seems to have its own brewery, and two of the best beers in England come from the heart of the Cotswolds — Donnington and Hook Norton. Donnington brewery looks like a manor house. Hook Norton is a steaming monster at one end of a handsome village, with equipment nigh on a century old.

In both countries, the pub *is* the village. You may end up stoned, but that isn't the object of the exercise. Close the village pub, and you close the village, which is what Watney's found a few years ago in Norfolk. Germany, again, has a solution here, because there are few villages without a small factory of one sort or another, so the population doesn't drain away. Adnams of Southwold, in Suffolk — another splendid pint — recognised the pub's essential role (applied social remedies are not the same thing at all) and have deliberately kept their pubs going.

Are the planners prepared to do their bit, by bringing industry back into the countryside? Small-scale industry, well-designed industry, but, above all, jobs. If they don't, the country pub will become a museum-piece, dependent on weekend tourists and holiday-makers — the motorway café in a prettier setting. The English pub depends on a steady balance, not famine-or-flood. This balance can no longer occur naturally; it has to be helped. Factories in the deep countryside and Green Belts near the towns are part of the same equation.

For, as a result of London's Green Belt, some of the best *country* pubs are within 30 miles of Westminster. Derided Surrey, that you flash through on the way to Gatwick and the Costa Whatsit, has quite a few. Village pubs beside village greens on which village cricket is played. Tilford, near Farnham, for one. Leigh, near Dorking, for another — this with splendid beer from King & Barnes of Horsham, another brewery that got away from the big boys. An Artificial Balance? Sure, but so is cricket and the English landscape. God endowed us with brains: let's use them.

Yet for every fine pub in balance there is another — down the road or in the next village — that is a dump. The beer indifferent, the customers sunk in platitude, both local and transient. The contract broken. A village can become a prison, as bad as any concrete jungle.

The way out, for the village as well as the village pub, is steady transfusion. As steady as the pull on the handpump. The village is dead, long live the village. Not what you dreamt of, not what the villagers may think at the time. But new blood, regardless.

So my final selection for a country pub is in the middle of the Black Country. The Glynne Arms is its official name, but everyone knows it as "The Crooked House". You get there down a track, through a kind of jungle, between Dudley and Gornalwood. Geese peck at you on the way in; you might as well be in the middle of Mexico. The beer — Banks's of Wolverhampton — is good. You are sober; everything is leaning, but it ain't your fault, lad. Subsidence acting on a timber frame has done the damage. Marbles will roll uphill on the window-sill.

The world turned upside-down? — or an unexpected sanity? Sanity, for me. Wildness in the middle of the densest of urban Britain.

Sunday Times, 9 July 1978

THE PUB THAT'S ABOUT TO BECOME A WETHERSPOON'S

Pete Brown

"Oh. Did you know that pub's about to become a Wetherspoon's?"

We're in town on the cider trail. The microbrewery tap we're drinking in doesn't have rooms, but another pub just round the corner does B&B for thirty quid a night. We've just told the regulars in the microbrewery tap that we're staying there. It's impossible to tell whether they think it's a good thing or a bad thing that the pub we're staying in is about to become a Wetherspoon's. Either way, they're very keen to tell us.

"There's a notice in the window," they say, nodding, and indeed there is - a Notice of Application for a New Premises Licence, on behalf of J D Wetherspoon plc.

The pub that's about to become a Wetherspoon's is bigger than it looks. There's only one bar open and the rest is in darkness, but if you were to explore you'd find another bar on the other side, that's set up to cater for diners who never come. And then, through a glass door at the back, there's another room as big as these two bars put together, where there is (or was) a carvery at weekends. The pub that's about to become a Wetherspoon's will make a perfectly good Wetherspoon's.

The pub that's about to become a Wetherspoon's is festooned with small plastic flags - Union Jacks and Welsh dragons hang from every beam. "They're left over from the festival," says one of the regulars at the bar. On every flat surface, and glued to every wall, there are posters offering you a free pair of sunglasses if you drink a certain quantity of Strongbow.

The barmaid in the pub that's going to become a Wetherspoon's is the reason most of the middle-aged male patrons drink here come here. She's very attractive, sexy enough to draw these men in, and approachable enough to make them think that maybe - just maybe - they might have a chance with her. There's a story doing the rounds that one of the regulars once took her home with him to meet his wife. Someone pointed out to him that this may have gone down better with the wife if it had been the other way round. But the pub that's about to become a Wetherspoon's doesn't feel like the kind of pub you take the wife to. It's not that it's unwelcoming to women — it's as welcoming to them as it is to anyone — it's just that it's obviously a place men come to get away from their wives.

The pub that's about to become a Wetherspoon's is close to the place where a five year old girl just went missing. Posters are everywhere - the ones you've seen on the news, and others featuring different photos of the little girl. It's on people's minds. Maybe it's one reason the town we're in feels like a ghost town. No one feels like going out. There's a depressed tension in the air.

"I'm going to go up there tomorrow to see if I can be of any help," says the attractive barmaid.

"What can you do?" asks one of the regulars.

"I don't know, but you've got to show willing, haven't you?" says the barmaid.

The 63-year-old retired property developer is one of the regulars who thinks he stands a chance with the attractive barmaid. He offers to accompany her to the cellar to change a barrel. He makes it sound sinister rather than flirtatious, but he doesn't mean to.

He tells us about the house clearance he just did where the tenant had been a chronic hoarder. He kept his own bodily fluids in bottles. Even kept his own shit. "We haven't found his nail clippings yet, but they must be there somewhere," he says.

The attractive barmaid rolls her eyes. "He tells that story to everyone who comes in," she says. "We had a nice couple in the other night who'd just had their dinner, and they turned round and walked out again."

The 63-year-old retired property developer doesn't realise that one reason he will never stand a chance with the barmaid is that he keeps telling his house-clearance stories.

The pub that's about to become a Wetherspoon's has a font on the bar with taps for draught wine. There are also branded taps for Strongbow, Blackthorn, Cobra, Carlsberg, Tetley's Cask, Worthington Creamflow, Tetley's Smooth, Pepsi, and a naked handpump with "Bank's Sunbeam" written in biro on a fluorescent yellow starburst Sellotaped to it.

The Carlsberg is undrinkable, but the attractive barmaid happily swaps it for a Cobra.

"My nose got split last Friday," says the attractive barmaid. "I've had my lip split before. They don't realise when they do it that they've just earned a criminal record and lost their jobs."

The 63-year-old retired property developer says he can't go home because his wife has guests round, and she doesn't want him embarrassing her because he's drunk. So he stays here, talking politics. The elderly man who goes to the microbrewery tap first and then comes here and sits alone, smart in his suit and tie, every night at the same time in the same seat, disagrees scornfully with everything the drunk property developer says, like a call and response catechism.

"These two do that every night," says the barmaid.

There's still a jukebox in the pub that's about to become a Wetherspoon's. Not enough pubs have jukeboxes these days. But tonight the jukebox is switched off, because the TV in the corner is on. It's switched to BBC4, which is showing a programme about the life and work of Norman Wisdom. Clips of him pratfalling, clips of him meeting the Queen, interspersed with ageing comedians and TV executives talking about what a gifted comic he was.

"Whass'on the tellee?" asks one of the regulars.

"Norman Wisdom," replies the attractive barmaid. She stares at the screen for a while, then asks, "What was he, a philosopher?"

"No, he was a comedian," replies the regular.

'Well 'e can't have been that funny, I've never heard of him," says the attractive barmaid.

The pub that's about to become a Wetherspoon's stays open late. When the property developer and the smartly dressed elderly man leave, we're the only customers in the bar. The attractive barmaid takes a seat and chats to us, and then three young guys come in for last orders, and she tells them how long they have to drink up.

It's late, and I call it a night. And as I go upstairs to my room, I wonder if — when Wetherspoon's finally do take over this pub, and they change some things and leave other things the same — I wonder if they'll rename it the Moon Under Water?

petebrown.blogspot.co.uk, October 2012

A Fine Excitement In A Quiet Country Life

Robert Louis Stevenson

His stories were what frightened people worst of all. Dreadful stories they were — about hanging, and walking the plank, and storms at sea, and the Dry Tortugas, and wild deeds and places on the Spanish Main. By his own account he must have lived his life among some of the wickedest men that God ever allowed upon the sea, and the language in which he told these stories shocked our plain country people almost as much as the crimes that he described. My father was always saying the inn would be ruined, for people would soon cease coming there to be tyrannized over and put down, and sent shivering to their beds; but I really believe his presence did us good. People were frightened at the time, but on looking back they rather liked it; it was a fine excitement in a quiet country life, and there was even a party of the younger men who pretended to admire him, calling him a "true sea-dog" and a "real old salt" and such like names, and saying there was the sort of man that made England terrible at sea.

Treasure Island, 1883

IN THE CHALICE

Jaroslav Hašek

There was only one guest sitting at The Chalice. It was the plain-clothes police officer, Bretschneider, who worked for the State Security. The landlord, Palivec, was washing up the glasses and Bretschneider was vainly endeavouring to engage him in serious conversation.

Palivec was notorious for his foul mouth. Every second word of his was "arse" or "shit". But at the same time he was well read and told everyone to read what Victor Hugo wrote on this subject when he described the last answer Napoleon's Old Guard gave to the British at the Battle of Waterloo.

"Well, it's a glorious summer!" said Bretschneider, embarking on his serious conversation.

"Shit on everything!" answered Palivec, putting the glasses away into a cupboard.

"It's a fine thing they've done to us at Sarajevo," said Bretschneider with a faint hope.

"Which Sarajevo?" asked Palivec. "Do you mean the wine cellar at Nusle? They're always fighting there, you know. Of course it's Nusle."

"At Sarajevo in Bosnia, Mr Palivec. They've just shot His Imperial Highness, the Archduke Ferdinand, there. What do you say to that?"

"I don't poke my nose into things like that. They can kiss my arse if I do!" Palivec replied politely, lighting his pipe. "Nowadays, if anyone got mixed up in a business like that, he'd risk breaking his neck. I'm a tradesman and when anyone comes in here and orders a beer I fill up his glass. But Sarajevo, politics or the late lamented Archduke are nothing for people like us. They lead straight to Pankrác."

Bretschneider lapsed into silence and looked disappointedly round the empty pub.

"Hallo, there used to be a picture of His Imperial Majesty hanging here once," he started up again after a while. "Just where the mirror hangs now."

"Yes, you're right," Palivec replied. "It did hang there, but the flies used to shit on it, so I put it away in the attic. You know, somebody might be so free as to pass a remark about it and then there could be unpleasantness. I don't want that, do I?"

"In Sarajevo it must have been a pretty ugly business, Mr Palivec."

This crafty direct question evoked an extremely cautious answer from Palivec: "At this time of the year it's scorching hot in Bosnia and Herzegovina. When I served there, they had to put ice on our lieutenant's head."

"Which regiment did you serve in, Mr Palivec?"

"I can't possibly remember anything so unimportant. Bloody nonsense of that sort never interested me and I've never bothered my head about it," answered Palivec. "Curiosity killed a cat."

Bretschneider finally relapsed into silence. His gloomy face only lit up on the arrival of Švejk who came into the pub, ordered a dark black beer and remarked: "Today they'll be in mourning in Vienna too."

Bretschneider's eyes gleamed with hope, and he said laconically: "On Konopiště there are ten black flags."

"There should be twelve," said Švejk, after he had taken a swig.

"What makes you think twelve?" asked Bretschneider.

"To make it a round number. A dozen adds up better, and dozens always come cheaper," answered Švejk.

There was a silence, which Švejk himself broke with a sigh: "And so he's already lying with God and the angels. Glory be! He didn't even live to be Emperor. When I was serving in the army a general once fell off his horse and killed himself without any fuss. They wanted to help him back onto his horse, to lift him up, but to their surprise he was completely dead. And he was going to be promoted Field Marshal. It happened at a review. These reviews never come to any good. In Sarajevo there was a review too. I remember once at a parade like that I had 20 buttons missing from my uniform and they sent me into solitary confinement for a fortnight, where I lay for two days trussed up like Lazarus. But in the army you must have discipline, otherwise why would anyone bother at all? Our Lieutenant Makovec always used to say: 'There's got to be discipline, you bloody fools, otherwise you'd be climbing about on the trees like monkeys, but the army's going to make human beings of you, you god-forsaken idiots.' And isn't that true? Just imagine a park, let's say at Charles Square, and on every tree an undisciplined soldier! It's enough to give you a nightmare!"

"At Sarajevo," Bretschneider resumed, "it was the Serbs who did it."

"You're wrong there," replied Švejk. "It was the Turks, because of Bosnia and Herzegovina." And Švejk expounded his views on Austrian foreign policy in the Balkans. In 1912 the Turks lost the war with Serbia, Bulgaria and Greece. They had wanted Austria to help them, and when this didn't happen, they shot Ferdinand.

"Do you like the Turks?" said Švejk, turning to Palivec. "Do you like those heathen dogs? You don't, do you?"

"One customer is as good as another," said Palivec, "never mind a Turk. For tradesmen like us politics doesn't enter into it. Pay for your beer, sit down in my pub and jabber what you like. That's my principle. It's all the same to me whether our Ferdinand was done in by a Serb or Turk, Catholic or Moslem, anarchist or Young Czech."

The Good Soldier Švejk, 1923

THE GARDEN GATE, LEEDS

Simon Jenkins

Our journey starts a mile out of town, where, in an unfashionable suburb and surrounded by low-rise offices and seventies housing, lies the most beautiful pub in Leeds.

If the Garden Gate were in a fashionable suburb, or close enough to the city centre to be part of the regular crawl, it would be lauded like Whitelock's and the Adelphi and prized yet more highly. Tourists would flock to gape at this working museum and sip tentatively at glasses of traditional hand-pulled mild, Nikons clicking like grasshoppers. Guide books would have it on the cover.

But the Garden Gate hangs in downtown Hunslet, at the end of a concrete cul-de-sac, and hard-up to a charmless red-brick Job Centre. There has been a pub here since before Queen Victoria's reign, its name a reference to the nearby market gardens, a source of significant local income at the time.

It looks lost in its surroundings, abandoned, bewildered by change, though its community is essentially the same one it has served for centuries. The houses are newer, the pace of life a little quicker.

And it thrives. Not simply by being old, or beautiful, nor by having the most amazing unspoiled interior you'll find anywhere, but by continuing to be there for the people of Hunslet, and by serving them well.

The pub is a ceramic cathedral, from the ornate brown and cream tiled exterior, to the greens of the pub's long central corridor which divides little snugs, nooks and crannies from the two main drinking areas either side of a central bar.

Wood, mirrors and glass predominate in each room. The corridor is itself a gem, tiled from floor to ceiling, save for polished mahogany panels and panes of etched and decorated glass. The floor is an ornate mosaic; a tiled archway arcs over the corridor.

But it's the ceramic which makes this place truly special. It's only a part-romantic notion that these tiles are Burmantofts Faience, a relic of the time when the east Leeds suburb was famed for its pottery. The present building — a perfect example of late Victorian and early Edwardian architecture — dates from 1902, when production at Burmantofts was still in full swing.

The curving bar counter, tiled floors and mahogany back bar make the front room, the Vaults, an absolute treasure.

It is all these features which have won for the Garden Gate international fame, being ranked in one recent list as the third most important pub in the UK, behind Liverpool's dazzlingly ornate Philharmonic and Belfast's majestic Crown.

Even the cellar is tiled. In these bowels of white-faced brick is glimpsed another past; a time when every pub and club, factory and church, fielded teams of men who carried their proud names across the whitewash. The Garden Gate had a fearsome reputation for rugby league. One can imagine great hulks of working men, stirred to the cause and striding into battle, local honour at stake.

Beyond the barrels and crates of ale, arched doorways open onto the abandoned changing rooms, a forgotten shrine to these local heroes. A leather table, where once a masseur would have pummelled players back into shape, stands forlorn in its midst.

The showers, the lockers, the communal bath are all still there, fragments of this glorious past. Ghosts must hang here, echoes of these great men, stepping through the fine hot mist of the showers, nursing their wounds and cursing still.

They might find today's society bewildering, fractured and lost, but drifting upstairs for an after-match pint, there is much they would recognise about the Garden Gate.

It's perhaps ironic that it has taken a Londoner, landlord Mark Anderson, to properly embrace this sporting past. Boards display the proud history of the local rugby league team the Hunslet Hawks, as though this were the tiny professional club's own museum. Pride of place goes to memorabilia from 1938, and the day when 54,000 people were shoehorned onto the terraces of Elland Road to see them defeat Leeds in the Challenge Cup Final.

Mark has re-instated links to the local club. A minibus runs from here to Hunslet's home matches; a group meets here monthly to discuss the club's proud past; you can even buy match tickets over the bar.

Mark leases the Garden Gate from Leeds Brewery, who rescued the pub after some years of pitiful decline. He admits: "I walked in and fell in love with the place."

Where once were just lager fonts are now handpulls dispensing Leeds Best, Leeds Pale and Midnight Bell — the wonderful trinity of real ales which have gained such a hold on the affections of the city's drinkers these past few years. This was a warm Sunday evening, and the sharp and citric Leeds Pale was the perfect antidote to the muggy weather.

Mark has taken the Garden Gate back to the basics of good, keenly-priced ale, simple hearty pub food, and friendly welcoming staff which are the hallmarks of a great community pub.

This hasn't always been the case. Not every landlord has treated this drinking palace with the reverence it deserves, nor ensured its customers did so. Incredible as it seems now, even the city fathers once plotted to flatten the place, as part of an ambitious local redevelopment during the slum clearances of the sixties and seventies.

Thanks to a vociferous campaign, that crass move was resisted, and the Garden Gate remained as a red-brick monument to the past, while the new homes of "The Motorway City of the Seventies" mushroomed all around. That battle, to save this slice of history from the advance of the bulldozers, led to pub the eventually winning the listed status whose protection underwrites its long-term survival.

Those rugby players would surely approve.

The Great Leeds Pub Crawl, 2012

Pub

Julian Symons

The glasses are raised, the voices drift into laughter,
The clock hands have stopped,
The beer in the hands of the soldiers is blond,
The faces are calm and the fingers can feel
The wet touch of glasses, the glasses print rings on the table,
The smoke rings curl and go up and dissolve near the ceiling,
    This moment exists and is real.

What is reality? Do not ask that. At this moment
Look at the butterfly eyes of the girls, watch the barmaid's
Precision in pouring a Scotch, and remember this day,
This day at this moment you were no longer an island,
People were friendly, the clock in the hands of the soldiers
    For this moment had nothing to say.

And nothing to say and the glasses are raised, we are happy
Drinking through time, and a world that is gentle and helpless
Survives in the pub and goes up in the smoke of our breath,
The regulars doze in the corner, the talkers are fluent;
Look now in the faces of those you love and remember
    That you are not thinking of death.

But thinking of death as the lights go out and the glasses
Are lowered, the people go out and the evening
Goes out, ah, goes out like a light and leaves you alone,
As the heart goes out, the door opens out into darkness,
The foot takes a step, and the moment, the moment of
    falling
    Is here, you go down like a stone.

Are you able to meet the disaster, able to meet the
Cold air of the street and the touch of corruption, the
    rotting
Fingers that murder your own in the grip of love?
Can you bear to find hateful the faces you once thought
    were lovely,
Can you bear to find comfort alone in the evil and stunted,
      Can you bear to abandon the dove?

The houses are shut and the people go home, we are left in
Our island of pain, the clocks start to move and the powerful
To act, there is nothing now, nothing at all
To be done: for the trouble is real: and the verdict is final
Against us. The clocks go round faster and faster.
And fast as confetti
      The days are beginning to fall.

The Second Man, 1943

3

BEER PEOPLE

Give me a woman who loves beer
and I will conquer the world.

Kaiser Wilhelm

DAD'S BEER: THE WORST AND MOST IMPORTANT BEER IN THE WORLD

Mark Dredge

"Can I try some of your beer?" I ask, reaching a hand up toward my dad. He passes me the stubby green bottle. I can barely fit my small hand around the wet glass.

He is with my uncles and granddad. They all drink the same thing and I want to drink it, too. I might be seven years old but I want to be like the grown-ups.

I take a sip and I can still taste it now, somewhere in the farthest corner of my taste memory: icy cold, harshly fizzy, then a flavour I've never had before, like sucking a new penny, and then it hurts my mouth, as if it's just been hit by a frozen metal rocket. "YUCK!" I give it back to dad and run off and play.

That's the first beer I remember drinking.

If there was an award for worst beer in the world then it might go to "Dad's Beer as Tasted by a Seven-Year-Old." That beer is one of the most horrible-tasting things any child could ever have, worse than cough syrup, even worse than vegetables. But if there were a lifetime achievement award for the most important beer of all time then Dad's Beer would take that prize.

Even as a little boy, seeing the adults standing around and drinking made me see some importance to the beers in their hands. I see the green bottle, something that I know is called beer, and it's a symbol of grownupness that they all like drinking, so it must be good. So I keep asking for sips and keep giving it back with a scrunched up face saying "EURGH!"

"Why do you drink that?" I ask.

"One day you'll like it, too," says my dad.

He wasn't wrong. And back then I'm pretty sure he wouldn't have foreseen that over 20 years into the future he and I would be sipping sour beers in the cellars of a dusty old Belgian brewery or that we'd be on a road trip up the West Coast of America, where I'm still asking the same question: "Can I try some of your beer?"

The Best Beer in the World, 2015

A BOTTLE OF IRON MAIDEN

Adrian Tierney-Jones

Trooper is a 4.7% bruised-gold premium bitter with a delicate lemon note on the nose and a bittersweet character on the palate. It was designed by someone who had already been a bit of a whizz at fencing, writing the odd book and piloting airliners, though no *Strictly* yet — and is also the lead singer of mega-metallers Iron Maiden. An amiable alliance on the brewing floor between Bruce Dickinson and the venerable family brewery Robinsons of Stockport, where the only metal in the building is usually part of the brewing kit, Trooper is the monster (mash) hit, the gold record, the beer that has made Dickinson a cask beer hero, while bringing Robinsons and its beer to a whole new market.

According to the brewery's Brand Manager John Robinson, "We very quickly realised when we started brewing three times a day five days a week for the first time in our history that this was going to be *big*. The Maiden following is crazy! They have an incredibly loyal fan base, who are almost a massive sales force in their own right promoting the beer."

Even though Iron Maiden's name is on the label, it's Dickinson who has made the running with the brew; the band's founder Steve Harris famously had a pub in his house but, according to Dickinson, "he has never been a big ale enthusiast, ironically".

As well as being deeply involved with Trooper, Dickinson announced the winners at the Great British Beer Festival in 2014 and provided the introduction for 2015's *Cask Report*. According to Pete Brown, author of the *Cask Report*, "When I interviewed him for the launch of Trooper I was surprised by his beer knowledge. But on the official launch day at the brewery, I was astounded. The brewery had just been rebuilt, and I'd just written the script for the new brewery tour. Bruce got taken through that script once, and then insisted on taking about 40 journalists and industry types on the brewery tour and he had it down word for word, not just parroting it but completely getting it. I thought, 'Here's one of the biggest rock stars in the world, and I genuinely think he'd rather be working here, doing this.'"

Dickinson was involved with the beer from the beginning, as John Robinson explains: "He has been to the brewery on many occasions and is incredibly passionate. He's a very knowledgeable man in a lot of areas, including beer! He has designed this beer, naming the hops and malt he wanted to use. He gets on very well with our head brewer too, and has even got into the detail of how much CO_2 is in the bottle, so he is a detailed man!"

Dickinson can date his interest in cask beer to what seems like rather an enjoyable school. "I was very lucky that we had a mini beer festival at my boarding school. Beers included Ruddles County, Pedigree and Adnams amongst others, all from wood casks and served on gravity. I was hooked forever!"

This passion, which has survived through decades of superstardom, gigs all over the world and plenty of best-selling albums, served him well when it came to making Trooper. "The beer was a slow burn," he says. "I wanted to create something genuinely different, and that takes time. It was a bit of a beer seduction process. I had several I tagged as favourites: Fullers ESB, Wadworth 6X and Abbot Ale for example. I am a big fan of Belgian and similar French ales such as Affligem, Grimbergen and Leffe. A teeny bit of that crept in. I must say I am very chuffed at the number of lager drinkers who name-check Trooper as being an ale that they can cope with."

A second beer with Dickinson, Trooper 666, is the same Trooper recipe but brewed to a strength of 6.6%. Its name suggests a link with the lightweight Hammer horror-style imagery the band have always favoured, but it also refers to the number of people who charged at the Battle of Balaclava, which is what the song is about.

"Trooper 666 is flying right now," says Dickinson, "and I'm delighted. For me it fills the niche between a British and Belgian ale, without tasting like a barley wine. I am so pleased that people have embraced the concept. And in my honest opinion, it's best served chilled. As for other Robinsons beers, I love Unicorn. If it were served in my local I would drink it. But Old Tom for me was a revelation. Sublime." As for being a cask beer hero, he's pleased, but not boastful: "I just created something that felt right."

Beer magazine, 2016

A BEERHOUSE-KEEPER FINED FOR STORING WINE

An Excise officer appeared at the Sunderland Police Court some days ago, to prefer a charge of storing wine against

William Rickerby, the keeper of a beerhouse at Deptford, Sunderland. The officer stated that he found three gallons of port and sherry on defendant's premises, contrary to the statute, and he was thus liable to a fine of 50*l*. In defence, Rickerby said he had got the wine for the occasion of his wife's confinement. A mitigated penalty of 12*l*. 10*s* was imposed. It is just probable that beerhouse-keepers will soon be prohibited to marry.

Brewers Journal, 15 August 1870

THE PUB POET

Alastair Gilmour

Your pint takes a moment to settle, you make yourself comfortable and you savour its malt and hop elegance. You nod acknowledgement towards the pub's friendly faces whilst congratulating yourself on a fine choice of ale. So, what happens next?

You can read a newspaper, gaze at your phone, debate politics, talk sport, argue religion, eavesdrop on conversation, or idly scratch a hole in a damp beer-mat. You can slouch and stare and ruminate, or rustle annoyingly through a packet of cheese and onion. You can listen to poetry.

To what? Poetry. It has been part of the pub experience for far longer than Sky HD or pickled eggs. Like the live band or the weekly quiz, it's an added attraction and on a definite upward curve of popularity. Now, a familiar face on the North East of England pub entertainment scene has committed his wittily entertaining way with words to the printed page. Poet, singer, songwriter and Radio Newcastle regular Simma – aka Anthony Simpson – has launched his first collection, *Last Night I Married the Audience*, published by Newcastle-based Zebra Publishing.

The man described by Rod Clements of Seventies folk-rock band Lindisfarne (*Fog on the Tyne*, etc.) as "a big-hearted performer and true poet of the people", was invited to write the book after Zebra managing director Jeff Price saw Simma performing around Tyneside.

"He came along to one of our poetry nights at the Cumberland Arms in Byker," says Jeff. "He's a singer and songwriter but had never done anything with the spoken word. His songs are very poetic in structure and I suggested he came without his guitar and just bring his words. He then started writing his own poems about performing in pubs. They're a mix of serious, subtle, laid-back and in-your-face."

Simma's poetry is definitely not from the "moon" and "croon" canon: they're amazingly well-observed slices of life harmonising the highs and lows of performing in front of an audience with one-on-one relationships and personal feelings. Some are tender, others are downright hilarious, peppered with perceptive lines such as in "Daytime in Darlo": "A girl with a litre of oblivion sits grinning on the teacup roundabout." In "Backbone" he writes deliciously: "Your mineral water sparkled, sadly not your conversation."

Simma is originally from Cruddas Park in Newcastle and honed his communication skills as a mobile phone salesman and sales trainer. He now co-hosts the Saturday breakfast show on Radio Newcastle with Simon Hoban. "People in the West End of Newcastle are very communicative," he says. "They look after themselves by talking to each other – it's where Ant and Dec also came from. I learned to use words to help get into people's affections.

"I've done the bigger concert halls and venues like the Tyne Theatre, but there's nothing like a packed bar; you're not separated from the audience, you're in the room with people. There's something about little bars, it's where it all starts. I like to perform in places I'd like to go to: nice places, nice beer, nice people. You feel you're communicating with the audience when in you're in a pub, it's not, 'I'm the performer, worship me' — people genuinely want to be your pal, they buy you a pint.

"This is my first book and I'm really, really excited about it. It's a coming-together of all things I've ever done. If you've got words in you, you can write poetry — you can write poetry about drinking a pint of Mordue Workie Ticket. Pubs, poetry, having a few drinks, it's as old as it gets, it's prehistoric. Every place is different. The Maltings in South Shields is going to be different to the Ship in the Ouseburn Valley or the Bridge Hotel in Newcastle.

"I learned from Lindisfarne records — especially Alan Hull songs — and the Beatles, the Stones and the Kinks, people like that; it's very economical writing. One guy said to me, 'That can't be poetry — I rather liked it'. It's like your first time with malt whisky — try it, you'll like it."

Andy Hickson, manager of the Bacchus in Newcastle, has watched Simma perform as a singer and as a poet in several pubs, so he understands the value that live acts can bring. "It's another reason to go out to the pub," he says. "When Simma organised the Acoustic Circus nights at the Bridge Hotel you'd be able to see six acts for £3, so on a quiet Wednesday with little else happening you'd get 70 people buying a few drinks each.

"In fact, I've seen it being so full we were turning people away. You can cater for a younger crowd, and it's also a platform for exposure at a grass-roots level, with people like Becky Owen ending up getting record deals."

When you're putting words on paper, does it matter whether they're for singing and strumming along to, or is there another approach to writing poetry? Surely they're one and the same disciplines.

"Being a singer-songwriter is completely different from being a poet," says Simma. "The difference is not the singing. People expect other things from a poet, they expect participation. Look at some of the great song lyrics — "All Right Now", or "A-Wop-Bop-A-Loo-Bop-A-Lop-Bam-Boom". When you're writing poetry, every word has to have meaning; you can't just go sha-na-na if you can't think of something. And the quality of words in poetry is much higher, you're not as constrained by metre and rhyme, and you can express yourself better as there are more forms of poetry."

Being described by one of your heroes as a true poet of the people must be enormously satisfying, so what happens next?

Simma says: "I know when to play working-class and when to go, 'I'm on the wireless, you know'."

Cheers, October 2011

GOOD PEOPLE
DRINK GOOD BEER

Jeff Evans

A Friday evening in a provincial English town. The town hall clock chimes seven, signalling the start of the weekend social round. The big pub in the market square is not one I frequent, but tonight — ever daring — I decide to check out what passes for entertainment in this particular watering hole.

Trade is slow at this early hour. There are a few couples picking over a rather drab-looking bar meal and a cluster of noisy drinkers hogging the bar, their physical presence and foghorn voices providing an intimidating barrier to service. Nevertheless, I press my way cautiously through the crowd and run my eye over the pump clips.

With a view to supping a few pints, I opt for a Brakspear Bitter. I like the depth of character this has for a beer of only 3.4% ABV. The rich malt and tangy hop flavours lure you in and the slight saltiness and teasing hints of butterscotch draw you back for another sip. Sadly, the beer is not in the best of conditions, suggesting that not many other people have made the same wise choice so far tonight.

The noise escalates as I edge my way out of the throng and head for a hopefully quiet corner. It's not quiet enough. I have direct eye-line to the bar but I could sit with my back to the counter and still know what's going on. The ringleader of the crowd is a big, brawny man in his thirties. He's had more than a few too many, his volume control has gone and — to borrow an old joke — he's swaying like an MFI wardrobe. His equally drunk girlfriend totters at his side. I assume it's his girlfriend from the way he keeps squeezing her left buttock.

With alcohol raging around his system, the man's oafishness becomes greater by the second and is raised to a new level when a young woman enters rattling a collection tin. It's Red Nose Day and she's doing her bit for the cause, no doubt thinking that, by volunteering for the early shift, she can avoid any aggro that might kick off among later revellers. It's a miscalculation. Approaching Oliver Reed, she is surely aware that she's in for a tough time and he doesn't disappoint.

Playing to the crowd, he begins a masterclass in boorishness, declaring his admiration for our unfortunate charity worker's curvy figure. Whipping out his wallet in a display of fake largesse, he extracts a £10 note and teases the collection tin with it. Just as he reaches the moment of penetration, he withdraws and, provocatively waving his financial potency in front of the girl's face, decides to make an estimate of the size of her bosom. 44 DD, he reckons, but he just needs to have a quick feel to make sure. The affronted woman recoils, protectively pulling her coat tightly about her. Realising from the sudden silence that he has overstepped the mark, the clown breaks out into embarrassed laughter, which is sycophantically echoed by his glassy-eyed cronies. Then, staggering forward again, he crumples the banknote into the collection tin anyway. He's only joking: the money's going in. That's how generous I am. The bravado continues.

The girl hastens away, muttering hollow thank you's, while the crowd guffaws in unison and more drinks are consumed. I don't know what exactly is in our friend's glass, but the blue colour tells me it's not beer. My pint is nearly empty and I'm glad to leave behind this dispiriting experience. I've seen numerous customers come and go, chased away by the drunken antics at the bar and witnessed glum staff stand indifferently by as the situation worsens. The pub has been rendered soulless, the atmosphere brittle and hostile. That's not what I've been looking for on my evening out.

I drain my glass and head back out into the night. My experiment with a different venue has failed and now I need to make up for lost time. Quickening my step, I make a beeline for the best beer house in town, a Fuller's pub alongside the canal. The prices are higher here but I know that I'll get an interesting beer served in excellent condition. I'll also, hopefully, be able to relax in a more hospitable environment.

There are four cask ales on the bar, plus some decent continental beers on tap and a small selection of bottled beers. I opt for the guest beer, a local ale from a microbrewery ten miles up the road. It's fresh and hoppy, bursting with bitter citrus fruit and zinging with natural effervescence, a crisp, clean beer that you are happy to let wallow on your tongue.

I find a seat at the end of the room. I like a seat with a view. When you're drinking on your own, bar-watching becomes compulsive, and I want to see just how different things are from the last place. It is immediately obvious that I am on another planet.

As in the previous pub, there are plenty of voices ringing through the air. But, far from being superficial, coarse and aggressive, this is the sound of happy chatter, of people having wholesome fun, catching up with old friends and chewing the fat with partners and colleagues. The sparkle of the beer in my glass is mirrored in the mood of my fellow drinkers. There's a spring in their step as they approach the bar and, after placing their orders, they fairly skip back to their tables with their drinks. Where the way through becomes tight, a polite "Excuse me" is reciprocated with a soft apology for having stood in the way in the first place.

Conversation is clear and easy to pick out. The language is bright rather than colourful; opinions are thoughtfully expressed rather than ignorantly slurred. Where there is laughter — and there is plenty of it — it is genuine, not the ugly braying I heard earlier. Most significantly, people are smiling, appreciating each other's company, all bathed in that lovely, gentle glow that only a great pint of beer can bring.

Not everyone, I admit, is drinking beer, but beer is definitely the leading currency. Quality ales, well kept and professionally served in clean, appropriate glassware, are the hallmark of this pub, and such qualities immediately instil a sense of well-being in the customer. Here, you're not parting with money: you're buying into a genuinely pleasurable experience. You appreciate it in an instant and it lightens your mood.

It is a joy to witness so many people shrugging the worries of the week off their shoulders and to understand the part that beer plays in the process. It's a role that only a few intoxicants can play. Others brutalise and demean their users, but beer, with its modest strength, big, complex flavours and uniquely satisfying quantities, stands apart.

The contrast between my two pub experiences that Friday evening could hardly have been clearer had Hogarth himself been there to sketch both scenes. I saw sad, sour people that base alcohol had inflated into cartoon social pariahs, and I rubbed shoulders with cheerful, vibrant people whose love of beer clearly brings them so much happiness that it spreads beyond their own souls and out into the wider world.

"Good people drink good beer" is a famous quote from the controversial American author Hunter S. Thompson. It's a perceptive point but one that, for me, also works in an inverted way.

I'd argue that good beer actually makes good people.

www.insidebeer.com, 2012

THE BONA FIDE TRAVELLER

I have been much exercised in my mind, says *The Hornet*, on the *bona fide* traveller question. Police, publicans, magistrates, and the public themselves all seem to be at a loss to define what a *bona fide* traveller really is. I have pondered the question, therefore, for some time, and slept over it several nights, carefully putting a copy of the new Licensing Act under my pillow on each occasion; and, in the end, I have drawn up a series of questions which I propose shall be answered by any one applying for refreshments at a public house during prohibited hours on the Sabbath. If this does not settle the dispute finally, I must leave it to be settled when the House of Commons resumes its sittings in February. These are the QUESTIONS: —

1. Where do you live when you are at home?
2. If you live there, why are you here now?
3. Have you a railway-ticket, if so, how many and how much?
4. What is your wife's maiden name? Also state if your name is duly marked on your shirt collar.
5. Have you ever had the measles?
6. Did you have salt bacon or herrings for breakfast?
7. Have you ever been out of England? If so, how far?
8. Did you ever discover any one, or write a book of travels?
9. State your opinions briefly on the Permissive Bill.
10. Give lucidly your reasons for not bringing some beer in your pocket.
11. Why are you not at some place of worship?
12. Have you ever put up at an hotel? If so, can you ever put up with one again?
13. Do you inculcate temperance principles against your neighbours?
14. On your honour, would not filtered water suit your case?
15. Will you promise this shall not happen again?

There, I think after all the above questions have been thoroughly answered in writing by the professed traveller, he may be admitted to the bar; and then, upon his writing his name and address in a book and kissing the new Licensing Act,

I would advise that he may safely be served with refreshment by the landlord.

Brewers' Guardian, 22 October 1872

BEING KEITH VILLA

Stan Hieronymus

Guess who made a beer with Chardonnay juice almost 20 years ago? The same guy who invented Blue Moon. Meet Keith Villa, the mind behind the "craft" side of MillerCoors.

Deep in the belly of the largest single-site brewery on Earth, Keith Villa checked the map one more time. The tank he was looking for would be here on the fourth floor of Cellar 16. He stepped carefully over piping, walked through a stainless-steel hallway with walls stretching to a ceiling 20 feet above and found storage tank 16D12. It could hold 1,583 barrels (more than 49,000 gallons), and the gauge showed it was about two-thirds full.

A tag hung from a sample spigot. It read, "Vintage Blonde."

One thousand barrels is considerably more beer than the average American brewpub will produce in a year, but might easily be misplaced at the MillerCoors Golden Brewery just west of Denver. The facility has nine ageing cellars, eight with six floors filled with 24 tanks per floor. The ninth cellar holds 18 tanks on four floors and 12 tanks on two. That's 1,248 lagering tanks.

Earlier in the day, with a considerably smaller brewery behind him, Villa looked at an online version of a story in *Details* magazine about "four beer trends to try now." The first featured beer-wine hybrids and put his Blue Moon Vintage Blonde Ale front and centre. He read the description: "Unfermented Chardonnay juice amplifies the tang of this wheat beer, Coors' spin on the trend."

He sighed, repeated the final five words out loud and shook his head. "We tested it [its original name: Champagne-All Wheat] right here in this room — in 1995," he says. Villa put down a glass of an India Pale Ale brewed with juniper berries and nodded toward an adjoining table, perhaps remembering the face of a customer, and certainly the conversation:

"Is it beer or wine?"

"Do you like it?"

"Well, sort of."

How do you make a wood-aged Chardonnay beer or a spiced saison-red sour hybrid approachable? Have Keith Villa brew it. With Vintage Blonde, his oak-aged, Chard-infused wheat beer, he manages to inject a bit of must that beckons cellarers, a vinous quality that shouts to the wine crowd, and an unmistakable Blue Moon friendliness that makes the beer feel like home. Villa's sleeper, though, is Farmhouse Red, a completely sessionable sour saison/Flanders red hybrid that hits at the heart of the brewer's remarkable restraint. An injection of hibiscus makes the swallow fruity and sweet yet utterly floral; a dose of white pepper brings a little dryness and a zing in the nose. Add that to a tart cheek-bite and you've got a beer that in any other hands would be a beast; this, though, is totally understated — totally Keith.

A few months before, Villa had brewed a beer with peanut butter at the SandLot Brewery inside Denver's Coors Field, where he did test batches. "Everybody had the same response: 'That's not as disgusting as I thought it would be,'" he recalls. "These were extreme beers back when there really wasn't such a thing, and almost nobody liked them."

He put those recipes from the Nineties on the shelf and didn't look at them again until 2006. "When I rolled them out, it seemed like we couldn't make enough for GABF and our test outlets [the SandLot and Falling Rock Taphouse, down the street]," Villa said. He called the beer brewed with malted wheat and concentrated grape juice Chardonnay Blonde, later changing it to Vintage Blonde because the government wouldn't approve a beer label that included "Chardonnay." It has won five Great American Beer Festival and World Beer Cup medals.

The peanut butter beer is so popular at GABF that they post what time it will be tapped, and by the time it's poured, the waiting line may be wrapped around itself. "I tried Jif, Skippy, Peter Pan and even freshly ground organic peanut butter from Alfalfa's Market," Villa says. "I even tried blends of peanut butter, almond butter and cashew butter. A version made with sunflower nut butter was called PeaNot Butter Ale for the GABF."

Blue Moon packaged Vintage Blonde Ale for the first time in 2011, testing it in 750ml bottles in limited markets. The 1,000-barrel batch Villa visited shortly before it was released in June 2012 didn't seem like much beer amid all those other ageing tanks in Golden, but there was enough to distribute nationally.

"We're not looking for it to become the next Blue Moon White," says Libby Mura of MillerCoors. Blue Moon sold 1.4 million 31-gallon barrels of Belgian White in 2011, more than any American wheat beer ever, and more than Samuel Adams Boston Lager, Sierra Nevada Pale Ale or New Belgium Fat Tire. Mura's title, marketing director for craft brands, introduces the elephant in the room. According to the way the Brewers Association, the organization most of America's 2,000 breweries belong to, defines "craft brewery" and "craft beer," Blue Moon and its brands are not "craft."

Blue Moon is a subsidiary of MillerCoors, a joint venture between Coors Brewing and Miller Brewing formed in 2007. The company brews the Blue Moon sold in the United States in three facilities: in 400-barrel batches at its Golden Brewery; in 800-barrel batches in Eden, NC; and in 10-barrel batches at the SandLot Brewery. "On a good day, if everything is going right and both breweries make their best beers, they'll be the same," Villa said a few years ago, at the time comparing Belgian Whites brewed at SandLot and the Eden brewery. "SandLot sometimes has a little too much clove (character), sometimes a bit too much spice. Eden is not as artisanal as SandLot. They are a production brewery. They make the beer the same time after time. That's what they do."

Arguing about what otherwise constitutes "craft" makes for popular sport on Internet discussion boards and in pubs. Villa chooses not to play. "We don't pay attention to those definitions," Villa said. "To me, it's always about your customers. You don't want them having a bad experience with your beers."

He may not focus on the definition, but he does read, and he noticed earlier this year when a *Denver Post* story intended to praise beers from AC Golden, which itself is located within the Golden brewery, caught Blue Moon White broadside. The article focused on sour beers that AC Golden brewer Troy Casey is making, and leaned on Jason Yester of Trinity Brewing for expertise.

"His beers are extremely authentic, very, very Belgian in character," Yester said. "I heard a lot of criticism. 'It's just going to be another Blue Moon, a dumbed-down version of a white beer.'"

"When I see a fellow craft brewer talking like that . . . " Villa says, using a telling adjective. "I love his beers. I would never say his beers were dumbed down."

He explains just how he developed the recipe for the beer that became Blue Moon Belgian White. He points out, accurately, that it wasn't the product of a marketing group, nor a knock-off of some other Belgian wit. He based it on his experiences in Belgium while studying in Brussels, where he earned a PhD with high honours in brewing biochemistry.

"To me, the standard white style didn't have that nice, smooth flavour the American palate would be looking for," he says. Instead of using unmalted wheat in the recipe, which was common, he included oats — far less common. Rather than brewing his White with Curaçao, again common, he decided on Valencia and navel orange peels. "Really refreshing, marmalade with vanilla notes," he calls them.

"If you were to taste all the white beers in Belgium, and then you talk to each brewer and tell him how this one tasted different than that one," he says, "the brewers will tell you only theirs has the authentic taste. That's the way brewers are. They are very proud of what they make."

Villa grew up near Golden and went to the University of Colorado 20 miles up the road. He had never been east of Nebraska before Coors sent him and his wife to Belgium between 1988 and 1992. After he returned, he took charge of new product development at the brewery. "You name a fruit, I brewed with it. Any new malt, spice, herb, hop — I was brewing with it," he says.

In 1994, Coors assigned Villa and Jim Sabia, who worked in marketing, to launch a brand on a shoestring. They started without a name or a marketing budget and, among other things, had to find breweries to make Blue Moon under contract from 1995 through 1999, before the brand grew large enough to brew in a Coors facility.

Although Villa helped design the ten-barrel brewery that sits on the right-field side of Coors Field and used it to develop new recipes, that the SandLot opened at the same time Blue Moon launched was a coincidence. Blue Moon Belgian White was first called Bellyslide Belgian White, because all SandLot beers had baseball-related names, as some still do. (Villa has a Bellyslide Belgian White pennant hanging in his basement.)

MillerCoors renamed the space Blue Moon Brewing at the SandLot in 2008. "Our fans wanted a brewery they could visit," he says. He may visit once a week himself or once a month, depending on his schedule and what new beers are on the docket. "I'll write the recipes and give them to John [Legnard] and Tom [Hail]. They turn them into liquid, beer," Villa says. "Without John and Tom, all these ideas would still be papers on a desk."

SandLot keeps the stadium pub stocked with a range of beers, including Blue Moon White, during baseball season and sells draft beer to regional establishments year-round. Its beers, primarily the German-inspired lagers, have won three dozen medals at the Great American Beer Festival. "We enjoy doing things people tell us we can't," says Legnard, who has worked at the space-challenged brewery since it opened. The names of those beers — Most Beer Judges are Boneheads, Not Quite World Class and Clueless Beer Writer among them — are as popular at GABF as the beers are good.

Villa's new recipes usually go on tap as brewmaster's specials. A few days before the baseball season opened, he sat in the empty pub and tasted the first batch of his IPA brewed with juniper berries and distinctively floral-fruity American hops, Centennial, Simcoe and Citra. "The resin from the juniper berries is tough to balance," Villa says. "I wanted to make an IPA in a Blue Moon way, with an inviting twist."

"I'm not sure where a beer like that would fit in," Mura says. "I think it does have a place in our portfolio." She knows that American IPA sales grew 40 percent in the previous year. "If you'd asked me five years ago, the answer may have been 'No.' We feel there are a lot more avenues for us to explore now. I think Keith has a lot of foresight and that really benefits Blue Moon."

He understands when to put a recipe on the shelf, and when to give it another try. "Back in 1992, Coors didn't know quite what to do with me," he says.

Somebody figured it out.

Draft, October 2012

A Cool Drink Of Ale After A Hot Afternoon's Cricket

Hugh de Selincourt

"Oh no! That's all right; I'll stay here," said Sid, protesting. But Ted Bannister took one arm and old John the other, and he was dragged into "The Dog and Duck", not, it must be owned, too reluctantly. A friendly but vigorous argument ensued between John and Ted Bannister as to who should stand treat, which was won by Ted Bannister, John grumbling that he never knew such a chap.

"Go on, put that inside yourself, mate," said Ted, handing him a pint of old Burton, for which "The Dog and Duck" had a name.

Nothing is quite so refreshing as a long, cool drink of good old ale after a hot afternoon's cricket; each man took a long, appreciative draught after wishing each other, "Well, here's luck!" and then in silence allowed the pleasant effect of that drink to permeate quietly through him before enjoying another good pull at the big pewter mug. John's face was a study of happy comfort as he slowly tilted his pot and, emptying it, set it down on the counter, carefully drawing a deep, comfortable sigh. Beaming, he watched the others follow his excellent example and then said, as though inspired by a sudden novel idea of extreme brilliancy:

"How about another small one?"

The Cricket Match, 1924

ADAM

Richard Taylor

The first sign of Adam's arrival is the pause, as the door opens seemingly without reason. Then, slowly, a wheelchair prods its way carefully through the opening. Eventually, the empty chair is pushed into the pub by its owner — a stooped, white-haired man, dressed always in a blazer, jumper and shirt. Adam creeps across the threshold of the Stockbridge Tap in Edinburgh, instantly glancing over at the seat he always aims for.

The wheelchair is left next to a radiator, and Adam slowly walks the short distance to that seat, from which he can see pretty much the entire pub. Even before he's halfway through the door, the bar staff at the Tap have started pouring his drink and, as he carefully settles on the padded bench, one of them brings it over, leaving it on the table with an "Evening Adam."

Every drinking house has its regulars — those who come for the conversation, the convenience, or those who see it as a second home and almost never leave. Eighty years old, Adam is no usual pub regular, even if he does live nearby. He's a familiar sight as he slowly pushes his chair down the hill from the Stock Bridge, stopping to chat to anybody that recognises him along the way.

He chooses to come into the Tap, and then sits in that specific seat, because of a different reason: familiarity. Back in 1951, when he was working as an apprentice painter, Adam turned 18. As an impromptu celebration, his boss took him out for a drink on his birthday — the first time he'd ever tasted alcohol. They sat, for the first beer of his life, in that same seat. So since then, he has sat nowhere else.

Come rain or shine, weekday or bank holiday, Adam has shuffled his chair through the entrance of the Stockbridge Tap and taken his place. At first, it became a habit — but it has long since become a ritual — and now he is nothing less than a fixture. He has made the same trip every day for over fifty years. Only the occasional illness and the time the pub cellar flooded has prevented him from turning up (he had to go to a neighbouring pub then, and didn't like it).

Adam's seat is on a slight angle, in between a small table near the trapdoor to the cellar and two larger tables that are often pushed together when people come into the Tap for food. At my local pub too, before I knew who he was I'd often see Adam, incongruously shoved in the middle of a group of diners, chatting away or staying silent, depending on the company and how they reacted to him. I'd often wonder why he was there, when other tables were available.

But of course, to him, they aren't: he has his seat and his age ensures he gets to sit there every time he enters the pub. Even if every other table was unoccupied he would still make a beeline for the same spot.

So what if his seat is taken, though, and there's no way he can squeeze in? Archie, the manager of the Tap, chuckles at the suggestion. "He'd just sit on you, anyway."

There's another reason why Adam doesn't have an unbroken run of occupancy in the Tap. Just as the war was ending, he was sent to serve in Germany: "The Geordies, the guys from Liverpool, very friendly." When he returned, he moved to Granton, three miles north of Stockbridge. But since he retired and left the painting business, he's been heading to the Tap — in all its previous guises — every day at 6.30 p.m., without fail.

So why does he do it? I ask him, and he looks totally nonplussed. 'You never get any trouble here, everyone's very friendly,' he smiles. And that's it. To underline the point, every now and again he waves to another regular, creased hands held aloft as they walk past his seat on the way to the toilet. "He used to be a major in the army." "That guy's from Norway, nice guy." All of them say hello to him by name as they pass.

Back in the day, he can't remember what the pub was called. Beer was never more than sixpence. He points over his left shoulder, out of the window, at a small block of flats over the road. "I asked a girl out who worked in the firm, her mother lived there. We brought her in here for a drink." The next table is suddenly occupied by a group of women, exiled from a nearby all-star tennis tournament abandoned due to rain. "McEnroe was there!" Adam tells them as one returns from the bar with a round of gins. "You cannot be serious!!"

Adam then switches track instantly, and uses their presence to talk to all of us about how the Tap used to be, with the different rooms, and how the women enjoyed the comfortable lounge. I buy Adam a beer — these days, he only ever drinks Best shandy; half a pint of Belhaven Best, topped up with the same amount of lemonade. He has an early tea at home, heads to the Tap, and drinks three pints before slowly pushing his chair back.

Before taking every sip of the shandy I've bought him, he thanks me. Adam used to drink regular beer instead (and buys me one soon afterwards, despite my protestations), but cut down "on doctor's orders" after the whisky part of the famed Scottish half 'n' half became the most important component. "Over time, you'd forget the beer was there," he says. I ask if he liked the taste of beer, on his birthday in 1951.

Adam pauses, wrinkling his forehead, before smiling. "Oh, aye," he chuckles, reaching for his Best glass.

www.thebeercast.com, July 2013

TIME TO CHANGE

Melissa Cole

I'm writing this on Time to Talk day, a date dedicated to helping end the stigma around mental health, and it's prompted me to address some behaviour in the industry that has recently set my teeth on edge around its attitude towards men (yes, you read that right). First up is serial sexism offender Marston's.

Just a few days ago the brewery decided to post on one of its social media channels an image of a pint of Pedigree over which it ran the slogan "There's no strong beer, only weak men". Apart from the obvious implication that only men drink beer, are they are calling any man who wants to responsibly drink a low ABV beer without getting hammered "weak"? Are they boasting that Pedigree is "strong" and that you are a total wuss if you don't skull 14 pints a night? Not sure which incredibly crass, hyper-macho option to pick, but it's certainly interesting coming from a company that proudly stated in a 2014 Department of

Health Responsibility Deal Alcohol Network report that: "We have [also] reduced our national brand, Pedigree, from 5% to 4.5%. We plan to reduce Ringwood Boondoggle down to 4.2% and Scarecrow down from 4.6% to 4%, and Old Thumper down to 5.1% (from 5.6%)."

Well, at least they got the "no strong beer" bit right, even if they managed to miss the responsibility part by a country mile — and that's the issue here, it's utterly idiotic on so many levels, but the highest one is that it calls men "weak", and helps perpetuate this awful pigeon-holing of them having to be "strong" all the time.

And before you dismiss the issue as an old boys' brown beer problem, sorry, but the "craft" community is, in places, significantly worse. Step forward probably the worst offender I've seen in some time, and that's Manning Brewers, a new Cheshire brewery that thought it would announce its arrival to the world with a flagship beer called Man Up and the slogan: "Coming in your mouths this Friday".

And I do apologise if you're eating whilst reading this, but then gagging does seem the appropriate response to this horror. . . Cheap jokes aside, I am trying to make a serious point.

Being told to "man up" or "be a man" are, in my opinion, the most damaging phrases for men's mental health in the English language.

For starters, what does it even mean "to be a man"? Mostly it means the vigorous suppression of any expression of feelings and a massive fight to fit into stereotypes, whilst being told you can't communicate any misgivings about them; and, to be honest, it's also about society undervaluing anything perceived as feminine - and if you think I'm being melodramatic about this, then just watch *The Mask We Live In* by Jenifer Newsom of TheRepresentationProject.org and you'll see what I mean.

But it's not just one documentary that says to me we should be concerned about how we market to men as well as women; studies show that alcohol dependency is roughly three times more prevalent in men than women, and that it's used by many as part of a series of unsustainable self-management strategies when handling depression.

I'd like to boil it all down about why I am annoyed about behaviour like that of Marston's, Manning Brewers and, also, the use of tragic sexist branding by breweries like another new kid on the block, Wiley Fox with its Blonde Vixen, complete with fox with gravity-defying tits because, men, you will buy anything with boobs on it, right?

And here is my problem with stereotyping and sexism like this in beer, in two stark sentences:

Craft beer is mostly consumed by 25–34 year old men.

The single most common cause of death in men under 35 is suicide.

So, if you still don't think it's time to talk about the perpetuation of misguided hyper-masculinity and the damaging macho culture in beer, you're clearly not listening.

Ferment, March 2016

WOUNDED SOLDIERS AND DRINK

An illustration of one way in which wounded soldiers conceal the fact that they are wearing hospital clothes when they wish to obtain drink was given at the Kingston-on-Thames Police

Court, when Francis Bridger, a Kingston licensee, was summoned for serving wounded soldiers in hospital uniform. The defendant showed in the witness-box that it was due to wounded soldiers concealing the white collar of their shirts and blue tunics with khaki handkerchiefs, turning up the collars of their khaki overcoats, and pulling up their blue serge trousers and putting on puttees which they carried for the purpose. Thus disguised, they looked like ordinary soldiers in full khaki. The defendant nevertheless was fined £10 and £2 2s. costs.

Brewers Journal, 15 July 1916

BEER PEOPLE

Garrett Oliver

Not quite two years ago, I found myself hosting a beer dinner at a country club in the charming Alpine-style town of Blumenau in the south of Brazil. I was the guest of the Mendes family, brewers of the Eisenbahn line of beers, authentic German-style beers harking back to Blumenau's German immigrant roots. The dinner was sold out. The chef had been flown in from Sao Paolo, and the food was excellent. A bossa nova band, grooving hard enough to blow any New York group off the stage, played in the corner of the room.

Bruno Mendes, who works with his brother Juliano and his father Jarbas at the brewery, turned to me and said, "Life is beautiful, isn't it?"

"Yes, it is", I replied. I had another sip of excellent Brazilian *weissbock*. At the end of the evening, following Brazilian custom,

I had to hug and kiss all the guests as they left. My hosts had a chuckle at my expense, watching the comparatively stiff American deal with the outpouring of local warmth.

Nine days later, having emerged from the smoke sauna on the edge of a frozen lake north of Helsinki, I stood naked in the snow drinking Finnish *sahti* from a traditional wooden cup. My host, the *sahti* brewer Pekka Karainen, gestured to a hole cut through the ice. "Now we jump in," he said with a grin.

"Right. You first," I parried, but it didn't save me — in I went. It was February. You have no idea.

Beer is like that, it seems. Over the years I've experienced the hospitality of brewers, princes, abbots, chefs, bar owners and beer enthusiasts, and I never cease to be amazed at the bonding power of beer.

When I was a homebrewer in the 1980s, I worried that becoming a professional brewer would ruin everything I enjoyed about brewing, that beer would just become a job. Fortunately for me, I could not have been more wrong. I haven't had a boring day yet. I work with great people and we try our damnedest to brew great things. We try to brew the truth.

The brewhouse is a trapeze act — you drop from the bar and someone grabs you before you fall; you let go in thin air, and the yeast grabs your hands and swings you back up to the platform. How I ever thought that such a thing could fail to be thrilling, I can no longer remember.

Americans love the idea of the self-made man, the one pulled himself up by innate genius and sheer force of will. No doubt these people exist, but I'm not one of them. As a brewer, the truth is that Michael Jackson made me, Mark Dorber made me, Roger Protz made me, Mark Witty made me, Steve Hindy and Larry Lustig made me, and yes, I had a hand in this enterprise, too. Beer people make each other. When you let go of the trapeze bar, someone is always there.

Quite possibly that person is your competitor, reaching out a helping hand. If you don't have the humility to grab that hand, you will fall, and there may be no net. And you won't deserve one, either.

The everyday thrill of beer is all these things. It's not only making new beers, exploring new flavors, and conjuring the alchemy of the brewhouse. It's also the chance to share what you know and take in what others have discovered. It's the chance to show people something brand new to like. Think about that. Does it sound like a small thing? Well, it isn't. You don't find something brand new to like every day.

Beer, like music, or art, or any other great enthusiasm, is a journey. If you're an avid jazz fan, there was a time when you didn't know jazz. Then there came a day when someone played you your first Coltrane album, your first Miles Davis album, or maybe Louis Armstrong's Hot Fives. On that day, a little door swung open. You walked through that door, and on the other side was a better life. That's not a small thing at all. We, as brewers, as writers, as homebrewers, as beer enthusiasts, open that door for people every day. Many of the best beers in the world cost less than a latte at Starbucks. That's a small miracle.

My fellow brewers have welcomed me into their houses and their breweries all over the world, whether they be castles, mansions, shacks, smoke saunas or monasteries. I'm grateful for everything beer has given me, and I can only hope to be around long enough to give enough back. I've already been around long enough to know that my people – beer people – are the best people in the world. And that's a small miracle too.

All About Beer, 1 January 2007

4

THE BREWING OF BEER

We brewers don't make beer, we just get all the ingredients
together and the beer makes itself.

Fritz Maytag

ANGELA INHERITS
A BREWERY

Sir Walter Besant

The walk from Stepney Green to Messenger and Marsden's Brewery is not far. You turn to the left if your house is on one side, and to the right if it is on the other; then you pass a little way down one street, and a little way, turning again to the left, up another — a direction which will guide you clearly. You then find yourself before a great gateway, the portals of which are closed; beside it is a smaller door, at which, in a little lodge, sits one who guards the entrance.

Mr Bunker nodded to the porter, and entered unchallenged. He led the way across a court to a sort of outer office.

"Here," he said, "is the book for the visitors' names. We have them from all countries: great brewers from Germany and America, who come to get a wrinkle. Write your own name in it too. Something, let me tell you, to have your name in such noble company.

"Ah! It's such a shame for such a property to come to a girl — a girl of twenty-one. Thirteen acres it covers — think of that! Seven hundred people it employs, most of them married. Why, if it was only to see her own vats, you'd think she'd get off her luxurious pillows for once, and come here."

They entered a great hall, remarkable, at first, for a curious smell, not offensive, but strong and rather pungent. In it stood half a dozen enormous vats, closed by wooden slides, like shutters, and fitting tightly. A man standing by opened one of these, and presently Angela was able to make out, through the volumes of steam, something bright going round, and a brown mess going with it.

"That is hops. Hops for the biggest Brewery, the richest in

all England. And all belonging to a girl, who, likely enough, doesn't drink more than a pint and a half a day."

He led the way upstairs into another great hall, where there was the grinding of machinery, and another smell, sweet and heavy.

"This is where we crush the malt," said Mr Bunker — "see!" He stopped, and picked out of a box a great handful of the newly-crushed malt. "I suppose you thought it was roasted. Roasting, young lady," he added with severity, "is for Stout, not for Ale."

Then he took her to another place, and showed her where the liquor stood to ferment; how it was cooled, how it passed from one vat to another, how it was stored and kept in vats; dwelling perpetually on the magnitude of the business, and the irony of fortune in conferring this great gift upon a girl.

"I know now," she interrupted, "what the place smells like. It is fusel oil." They were standing on a floor of open iron bars, above a row of long covered vats, within which the liquor was working and fermenting. Every now and then there would be a heaving of the surface, and a quantity of malt would then move suddenly over.

"We are famous," said Mr Bunker, "I say we, having been the confidential friend and adviser of the late Mr Messenger, deceased; we are famous for our Stout; also for our Mild; and now we are reviving our Bitter, which we had partially neglected. We use the Artesian Well, which is four hundred feet deep, for our Stout, but the Company's water for our Ales; and our water rate is two thousand pounds a year. The Artesian Well gives the Ale a grey colour, which people don't like. Come into this room now," — it was another great hall covered with sacks. "Hops again, Miss Kennedy; now, that little lot is worth ten thousand pounds — ten — thousand — think of that; and it is all spoiled by the rain, and has to be thrown away. We think nothing of losing ten thousand pounds here, nothing at all!" — he snapped his fingers — "it is a mere trifle to the girl who sits at home and takes the profits."

Then they went into more great halls, and up more stairs, and on to the roof, and saw more piles of sacks, more malt, and more hops. When they smelt the hops, it seemed as if their throats were tightened; when they smelt the fermentation, it seemed as if they were smelling fusel oil; when they smelt the plain crushed malt, it seemed as if they were getting swiftly, but sleepily, drunk. Everywhere and always the steam rolled backwards and forwards, and the grinding of the machinery went on, and the roaring of the furnaces; and the men went about to and fro at their work. They did not seem hard worked, nor were they pressed; their movements were leisurely, as if beer was not a thing to hurry; they were all rather pale of cheek, but fat and jolly, as if the beer was good and agreed with them. Some wore brown-paper caps, for it was a pretty draughty place; some went bare-headed, some wore the little round hat in fashion. And they went to another part, where men were rolling barrels about, as if they had been skittles, and here they saw vats holding three thousand barrels; and one thought of giant armies — say two hundred and fifty thousand thirsty Germans — beginning the Loot of London with one of these royal vats. And they went through stables, where hundreds of horses were stalled at nights, each as big as an elephant, and much more useful.

In one great room, where there was the biggest vat of all, a man brought them beer to taste; it was Messenger's Stout. Angela took her glass and put it to her lips with a strange emotion — she felt as if she would like a quiet place to sit down and cry. The great place was hers — all hers — and this was the beer with which her mighty fortune had been made.

"Is it?" she asked, looking at the heavy foam of the frothing stout; "is this Messenger's Entire?"

"This is not Entire", he said. "You see, there's fashions in beer, same as in clothes; once it was all Cooper, now you never hear of Cooper. Then it was all Half-an'-arf — you never hear of anyone ordering Half-an'-arf now. Then it was Stout. Nothing would go down but Stout, which I recommend myself, and find it nourishing. Next, Bitter came in, and honest Stout was despised; now, we're all for Mild. As for Entire, why, bless my soul! Entire went out before I was born. Why, it was the Entire that made the fortune of the first Messenger that was — a poor little brewery he had, more than a hundred years ago, in this very place, because it was cheap for rent. In those days they used to brew strong Ale, Old and Strong; Stout, same as now; and Twopenny, which was small beer. And because the Old Ale was too Strong, and the Stout too dear, and the Twopenny too weak, the people used to mix them all three together, and they called them 'Three Threads'; and you may fancy the trouble it was for the pot-boys to go to one cask after another, all day long — because they had no beer engines then. Well, what did Mr Messenger do? He brewed a beer as strong as the Three Threads, and he called it Messenger's Entire Three Threads, meaning that here you had 'em all in one, and that's what made his fortune; and now, young lady, you've seen all I've got to show you, and we will go."

All Sorts and Conditions of Men, 1890

BREWDOG: DIACETYL MACHINE AND ALL

Adrian Tierney-Jones

There's a machine for testing diacetyl, snug and secure in the cabin-sized, glass-fronted laboratory that looks out onto the cavernous, cathedral-like (vast and open as in the starkness of a great northern European space for worship rather than one in the south, Malaga for instance) brewing hall with its steel ribs reaching out and holding up the sky (and keeping out the sky). There's a machine for blasting more hops into the FVs: silvery, towering cylinders sitting out in the grey, chilly morning that is the colour of mud-streaked chalk — a hop cannon, says Martin Dickie. "Who wants to climb to the top?" asks James Watt, and a couple of hardy souls clamber up the steel ladders. Back inside the cathedral of a brewing floor there are miles of metal pipes through which beer flows; there is the hum of machines and there is the clang of metal and there are the voices of brewers as they get on with their day's work.

Then there is the clinking, chinking, ice-and-a-slice-in-a-glass-of-G&T music of bottles of Jack Hammer as long lines twirl their way around the bottling line (Peter West really should be here). The bottles slow down, gather together, like wildebeest on one of their great treks, or a crowd being funnelled into the turnstiles when Saturday comes, crowding together for comfort, and then they are bedded down, 24 bottles intimate in a cardboard box, no street drinkers these.

The brewing floor of BrewDog is noisy and purposeful, a vast conclave of stainless steel cardinals gathering together to elect the next beer pope. The noise is reminiscent of the 1980s band Collapsing New Buildings and thoroughly melodic in the effect it has on the brain. "Come inside a container," says BrewDog's James Watt; quietly spoken, slightly shy, it seems to me, nothing like the reprehensible, irresponsible pranksters that some have suggested. "Come inside where we leave Sink The Bismarck." There's a wreath of cold air: it's -25°C inside here, gone in 30 seconds.

I've always liked BrewDog. I've always liked the swagger, the up-yours and even the wind-up gramophone of slight hysteria, but in recent years they seemed to have slipped off my radar: the punk aesthetic was becoming tiresome (after all, punks grow up, or in my case grow their hair a little longer). Hardcore is my favourite beer of theirs, and I've always enjoyed visiting the bars in Camden and Bristol; I pick up Punk when I see it and Dead Pony is rather special. But . . . I have felt divorced from them, felt that they were doing lots of different beers, crowd- sourcing and collaborations amongst them (didn't enjoy the Flying Dog one for instance, which I felt disappointed with in a bar in Rimini), dude-ing it up, and there was nothing substantial for me to think or drink about. There's also the revivalist nature of the fans. I'm always suspicious of evangelical movements, whatever the nature. It is just beer, after all.

But . . . when the invitation came to fly up north to Aberdeen and spend a day in their company, drink their beers, see the new (13 months old) brewery, hear about their plans, visit their bar and eat at Musa, I said yes, even though there remained a cynical part of me that asked my inner ethicalist (a rarely awaken kraken-like segment of me usually asleep in an Arcadian grove where everything is jolly nice): would it be a stunt? Would we (there were 10 of us, from the UK, Norway, Finland and France) be met by a man in a gorilla's suit on a bicycle with ten seats? Would we discover that the brewery didn't exist, and that it was a cosmic joke on those of us who dare to approach the unstoppable and bewildering bewitchment of beer with the same seriousness that other writers treat rock culture? On the other hand, this wouldn't be your typical corporate brewery trip where the PR type, eyes gleaming with a messianic beam of righteousness, would blab on forever why this brewery (or maybe it's that brewery or the brewery over there even) had finally understood craft — here, have a glass of our craft beer (re-badged and reborn and re-jigged with its own Grizzly Adams beard and aslant Tibetan prayer flat cap).

In the tasting room we go past friendly people doing the sort of jobs that all breweries require their people to do, whether craft, kreft or completely unaware of what point of the compass they should proceed; in the tasting room we gather, beer bottles popped, caps rattle-trapping on the table, glasses hustled by the quicksilver approach of beer. James Watt had sidled in earlier on, before our expedition onto the brewery floor, introducing himself (well, what was I expecting — Loki?), thanking us for coming in a voice that was mid-Atlantic Scots, and gradually warming to his theme: we make the beer we like to drink. Then Martin followed, a thicker Scottish brogue, slow and stately, deep, a ponytail in his wake.

And after the brewery tour we began tasting beer.

Punk IPA has its trademark pungent and arousing nose, peach and apricot skin (ripe and luscious after time spent in the sun); lychees, papaya, mangos trip off the tongue, while I pick up a gentle touch on the elbow of white pepper in the dry and grainy finish. Jack Hammer is a bigger beast, with the bitterness clanging away like an alarm bell announcing that the Vikings have just landed and all must fight or die. Dead Metaphors is the colour of a moonless night, smoky, coffeeish, chocolaty, both lean and creamy-smooth in the mouth, a counterpoint between the dark, dark, dark into which we all go and the soothing milk stout flurry of benevolent violins (for this we thank Richard Taylor and Rob Derbyshire).

"This is something new," says James Watt: AB15, an imperial stout with salt caramel and popcorn in the mix, a beer that has ruminated and contemplated time in both rum and bourbon casks before being blended together. It's vanilla, woody, velvety, rich and spirituous, sweet, caramel-like and a sly shoulder-barge-when-the-ref-isn't-looking of saltiness manifesting itself on the back of the tongue; there's an opulent, silk-sheets kind of sweetness, before there's a knock on the door of the five-star bedroom that the beer has become, announcing that dinner will be served, but do continue to linger with the beer; it's a multi-layered and complex-flavoured beer where flavour notes crash all over the palate like neutrons in a particle accelerator before coming together in a steady stream of all that vanilla, caramel, berry fruit, smoke, coffee and complete pleasure.

Later on James and a couple of others drive us to the original brewery in Fraserburgh, cold and closer to the sea than I would like to be, robust and rugged, experimental (white IPA, mango Berliner Weiss), friendly brewing staff. And it's then that you begin to realise how small and near the knuckle things were for BrewDog in the early years. Two men and a dog (the latter sadly dead – James Watt and I shared a few quiet moments talking about dogs), equipment cobbled together, tight-fisted banks, so perhaps you can see why they felt the need to act the way they did in those early years ("There are things we wouldn't do now," said James Watt). It got up the noses of the brewing industry, pissing off some pretty decent brewing people, but that's the past.

As we got into Aberdeen and drank beer at the BrewDog bar and then great beer and food matches at Musa I made up my mind: BrewDog are a force for good. They might not always get it right (my glass of Fake Lager had seemingly escaped the diacetyl machine, but the next one hadn't, so this was that great issue that effects all beer: dispensation); they are not in it for the short term (for God's sake, they're still in their early 30s); the beer often reaches heights that Buzz Aldrin would envy (though there have been lows that Dante Alighieri would have known about); and there's a force of nature about them that suggests they might sometimes get it wrong, but more often or not they will get it right.

www.maltworms.co.uk, February 2014

ABOUT CORONATION ALE

Graham Swift

In June 1911, during the preparations in Gildsey for celebrating the coronation of George V, amidst the hanging of flags, the building of bonfires, the arranging of floral mottoes and planning of banquets, my grandfather, the morose and unpopular brewer of the town, proposed to make his own contribution to the festivities by producing a commemorative bottled ale, to be called, appropriately enough, Coronation Ale; the first thousand bottles to be issued free, but no drop to pass any man's lips till the king was indeed crowned.

Though it had already passed, in a form known simply as "Special", my grandfather's lips. And perhaps too the budding lips of Helen Atkinson, my mother.

Warmed by patriotic zeal and softened by a mood of reconciliation (so, when it comes to it, the peevish brewer can say his God Save the King like any man), the townspeople chose to forget for a moment their differences with Ernest Atkinson. The jubilant day drew near. They cast their minds back to other times when they had been licensed to swill beer in a noble cause:

to the Diamond and Golden Jubilee Ales, even to the Grand
'51, and so to those halcyon days when the fortunes of the
town had bloomed. Had those days gone for ever? Could this
National Occasion — so Ernest Atkinson ventured, addressing
the Celebrations Committee, with no hint of politics but with a
curious glint in his eye — not include a local one? For was it not,
he pointed out, the glint becoming curiouser, almost exactly one
hundred years ago that Thomas Atkinson received, to the great
grudgingness (uneasy laughter amongst the committee members) of certain Gildsey factions, the Leem Navigation, thus
inaugurating the process by which this once obscure Fenland
town gained its place in the Nation — if not, indeed, the World?

What was in this Coronation Ale, offered in a dark brown
bottle of a shape narrower and more elongated than the beer
bottle of later days, with "Atkinson — Gildsey" embossed upon
it and a label bearing a large crown, centre, and a continuous
border of alternating smaller crowns and union jacks? Nectar?
Poison? Merriment? Madness? The bottled-up manias of His
Majesty's subjects?

Rest assured, it was no ordinary ale that they drank by the Ouse
while in Westminster crowds thronged, guns fired and the Abbey
bells pealed. For when the men of Gildsey jostled into The Pike
and Eel and The Jolly Bargeman to be amongst the privileged first
one thousand to receive their bottle gratis and to raise their glasses
in decent good cheer to toast the King, they discovered that this
patriotic liquor hurled them with astonishing rapidity through
the normally gradual and containable stages of intoxication:
pleasure, satisfaction, well-being, elation, light-headedness,
hot-headedness, befuddlement, distraction, delirium, irascibil-
ity, pugnaciousness, imbalance, incapacity — all in the gamut of a
single bottle. And if a second bottle was broached —

Waterland, 1983

THE EFFECT OF THE FRANCO-PRUSSIAN WAR ON THE DRESDEN BREWERIES

The first effect of the declaration of war, which took all Germany quite as much by surprise as any other country, was to create a panic in Dresden as well as in other cities, by which every description of funds and securities were seriously depreciated, and in fact became unsaleable at any price. But in a few days confidence was restored to a certain degree, and the values of shares in railways and other industrial undertakings partly recovered, though they are still considerably lower than before the crisis.

The Dresden brewery companies did not escape the general panic, and the value of their shares was greatly affected; but they have now so far recovered that the Waldschosschen shares have improved 9 per cent, and are now worth 139 per cent. Feldschlosschen have risen 20 per cent, and are now quoted 170 per cent; Felsenkeller recovered 11 per cent, and find buyers at 161 per cent; Medingen are 3 per cent better, and are held at 48 per cent; and Reisewitz improved $3\frac{1}{2}$ per cent, and are officially quoted at $98\frac{1}{2}$ per cent.

There is no particular reason why the shares of the Dresden breweries should be depreciated by the war, for on whichever side the victory may finally alight, the consumption of beer cannot be altogether set aside; and even should the French armies be enabled to advance so far into the heart of Germany, and hold military occupation of Dresden for any length of time, should they respect private property — as for the honour of France, there is every reason to believe they will — there must be a very considerable increase in the consumption of beer in the country, which of course can only tend to increase the profits of the Saxon breweries. In the meantime the late sultry weather has been extremely favourable for their interests, and given a great stimulus to the trade by creating an unusual degree of thirst and a corresponding demand for good wholesome beer.

The proposed congress of German brewers, that was to have been held at Dresden at the end of July, and of the preparations for which we gave our readers some account in a previous number, has of course been knocked on the head by the suddenness with which the war broke out, and has been postponed till more quiet times.

Brewers Journal, August 1870

VATS OF PORTER, WONDERFUL

James Joyce

As he set foot on O'Connell bridge a puffball of smoke plumed up from the parapet. Brewery barge with export stout. England. Sea air sours it, I heard. Be interesting one day get a pass through Hancock to see the brewery. Regular world in itself. Vats of porter, wonderful. Rats get in too. Drink themselves bloated as big as a collie floating. Dead drunk on the porter. Drink till they puke again like Christians. Imagine drinking that!

Ulysses, 1922

Pasteur's New Method
Of Brewing

The most eminent of French scientists (says the *British Medical Journal*) at this moment has taken out a patent, of which the avowed object is to slake his country's thirst for vengeance in a manner remarkable for its pleasing and profitable ingenuity. M. Pasteur has taken out a patent for a new mode of brewing beers, "applicable to mild and strong, brown or pale ales." In commerce he desires that his beer may be called "Bières de la Révanche Nationale," and abroad that of "Bières Françaises." M. Pasteur's process of brewing is founded on observations that contact with air is injurious to the manufacture of beer. He claims for his process that it makes more beer, better and stronger, from the same amount of material; that there is no need of cooling-vats, ice-houses, or store-cellars for his beer.

The notion of quenching the thirst of his countrymen for revenge in foaming tankards of unsurpassed home-brewed beer is eminently patriotic; and if M. Pasteur can drive Dreher from the market, conquer Bass, expel Viennese Lager Bier, and introduce the Bières Françaises in the Trink-Garten, he will have achieved a pacific triumph of which not even Prince Bismarck might be proud, and which he would not hope to rival.

Brewers' Guardian, October 1872

Relaxed

Frank Priestley

During the time I was working in the bottling laboratory I had been given the chance to visit Brew-X, the brewing exhibition that was regularly held in one of the large exhibition venues in London. Most of the production staff would be going, although in order to minimise disruption to the running of the brewery, people from the same departments would, as far as was possible, go on different days of the week. In other words, our visits would be "staggered".

Brew-X was an opportunity for the many companies that supplied the brewing industry with raw materials, plant or services to show what new innovations they could offer. It was their chance to strengthen links with existing customers and to forge new links with potential ones, all in a very convivial atmosphere. Since I was going to be travelling down alone, colleagues advised me that there would be a lot of drink about and that it would be quite an enjoyable session.

I was not disappointed. Not only were there several bars in the exhibition hall, but many of the exhibitors were offering "hospitality" on their stands. I got around as many stands as I could and accepted as much hospitality as I could manage and by the time I made my way back to the station for the return journey I was pleasantly relaxed. I was not drunk. Brewery people do not get drunk; they get "relaxed" (just as politicians get "tired and emotional").

The train back to Sheffield was not due for half an hour or so and as I sat on a bench waiting, the thought came to me that this had been my first visit to Brew-X, and if I was asked what I thought about it, I estimated that by tomorrow, I would not remember a single thing. So, in order to remedy this, I leafed through my crumpled copy of the exhibition guide and tried to remember which stands I had visited. I identified about five or six and then I wrote a few notes in the margins, describing what they had to offer.

About a week later, the Head Brewer sent a memorandum to all those who had been to the exhibition, requesting a report from each of us. He wanted to know what new developments had been on display and how these could be of benefit to our own brewery. He outlined five or six headings on which to base our reports. I frantically dug out my exhibition guide, which was by now, very crumpled, and found I was able to draft out a passable report. Those, almost illegible, spidery notes had succeeded in saving my bacon.

The Brewer's Tale, 2010

How Wild Is Your Beer?

Jeff Alworth

One of the best breweries I know is so obscure and out-of-the-way that most people living an hour and a quarter away, in Portland, don't even know it exists. It's named Solera, appropriately, after an equally obscure technique of nurturing wild ales. In an era of hops, the brewery does have one IPA, but mostly focuses on much more unusual styles of a kind that don't enjoy a mass audience. The brewer, Jason Kahler, doesn't seem to care about any of this. When he walks out the back of the brewery in tiny Parkdale, he has one of the best views of Mount Hood anywhere in Oregon, and the rows of orchards that fill the valleys provide him with a seasonal supply of beer-ready fruit as well as those wild yeast and bacteria that ferment his wild ales.

I visited him recently to learn about the solera technique that gave the brewery its name and how to adapt it for home-brewing. Before I'd even gotten to ask my first question, though, he posed one to me: "What's your philosophy about wild ales?" I stammered for a moment and then asked what *he* meant about a philosophy of wild ales. I had honestly never given it a lot of thought. "Well," he began, "a lot of people consider anything with *brettanomyces* or bacteria in it 'wild.'" If we were going to discuss wild ales, he just wanted to clarify what we were talking about.

Don't worry, this isn't going to be one of those pedantic nomenclature posts I occasionally lapse into. But it does bear mentioning that we don't have any good language to distinguish between a range of beers that are labeled variously "sour," "Brett," "spontaneous," or "wild." The real problem here is not the language but the confusion about what these beers are and how they're made. Our local NPR affiliate recently did a story where they conflated different practices illustrating the problem:

If you're tuned into the world of beer, you may be aware of sour beers — a loosely defined style that has been made for centuries but is gaining fresh appreciation in today's craft beer renaissance. Brewers make these beers by deliberately adding bacteria and, sometimes, wild yeast to the brew, then letting them age slowly. It sounds weird, but sours can be delicious — tart and earthy, and redolent of things like leather, fruit and wood. They're also very hard to make, requiring months or years of letting the beer gradually mature in the cellar.

But a technique that makes brewing sour beers fast and easy is trending across America — making sours much more affordable. The technique is called kettle souring, and it allows brewers to produce a mouth-puckering sour in about the same time it takes to make any other beer. The result can be generous pours of acidic, face-twistingly refreshing beer for the standard price of a pint.

Kettle-souring is a process in which brewers add *lactobacillus* to fresh wort to create an acidifying lactic fermentation. That wort can then be fermented with normal yeast, resulting in beers of varying tartness. It's entirely different than adding a culture of *brettanomyces*, which may take months or years to work its magic and which may add very little acidity in the process. And it's very different still from inviting native microbes into your beer naturally, to let them do the work without any help from lab-grown yeasts or bacteria.

Any of these processes can produce spectacular beers. The question Kahler posed, however, had less to do with the finished product than the process. Making beers with yeast and bacteria harvested from nature is an inherently dangerous business. Not only are you introducing unknown micro-organisms into your brewery, but you're also handing over control of your beer to them. "If you're getting [yeast] from a laboratory, how wild is it?" Kahler asked. "It seems like a pretty controlled process." And this is what separates Kahler and a growing number of wild-yeast wranglers from those who pitch cultures in order to maintain some level of control.

(Though even lab-grown cultures are dangerous. A number of breweries have been stung by the caprice of these little buggers, illustrating the risk. In 2010, Goose Island had some rogue *lactobacillus* get into Matilda, forcing a recall. The next year, Deschutes discovered that the Brett used in barrels of Dissident had migrated to those holding Mirror Mirror and The Abyss. And in 2013, The Bruery had a big enough problem with cross-contamination that it had to recall a number of beers and rework its brewery practices.)

If you wanted to boil the whole of modern brewing to a single goal, it's trying to gain as much control over the biochemistry of the brewing process — starting with keeping wild yeast *out* of the brewery. This approach seems fundamentally contrary to brewing wild, which requires the embrace of randomness. When I visited Cantillon back in 2011, Jean Van Roy — who is equal parts poet, philosopher, and brewer — put it this way. "It's never the same. Never. You never know what you will discover. That's why lambic is so fun. In French we have a sentence. We say, *tout est dans tout*. If I translate it: everything is in everything. In this brewery, everything is playing a role in the final product. Everything."

This is not the approach of the modern brewer; it's something closer to an alchemist — which Kahler acknowledged. "It's kind of magical in my head. There's obviously hard science behind it, but I don't understand all that science, and I don't think you *have* to understand that science." Although he has done some spontaneous fermentation in the lambic mode, Kahler's preferred method is inoculating wort with the yeast and bacteria that lives on fruit. Cherries and peaches are his faves, and he dumps in whole fruit to freshly chilled wort. "I don't worry too much about [it]," Kahler said, waving away concerns I raised. "Getting back to philosophy: that's something that you have to get over, your fear, if you're going to try these beers. You can't lose sleep over something like this."

Is there a difference between inoculated-wild ales and truly wild ales? There is. A Brett-aged beer will develop a lot of complexity as the wild yeast slowly creates different flavour and aroma compounds. Some breweries even add a cocktail of *brettanomyces, lactobacillus* and *pediococcus*, which creates even more complexity. But truly wild ales have something more. The biodiversity is much greater, for one. You're getting a greater range of yeasts and bacteria in a wild beer, including wild *saccharomyces* that conduct the initial fermentation. But even more than that, you're getting the taste of place.

Every strain of *brettanomyces* is different, and strains can vary even as close as a mile or two away. Last year, as part of the Beers Made by Walking program, Daniel Hynes, then of Thunder Island Brewing, put wort out in five different locations within Forest Park in Portland. He conducted spontaneous fermentations on each of them, wondering if, say, putting wort next to a nurse log or giant snag full of holes would produce different flavors than wort placed in new growth. And indeed it did — hugely. And that was just within the space of one patch of forest; imagine the difference ecosystems, climate regions, and local vegetation would have on beers fermented naturally in California, Iowa, New York, and New Mexico?

"You can get *brettanomyces* from the laboratory and you can get Brett from the air," Kahler says. "I love *brettanomyces*, I love *lactobacillus*, *pedio*. They're all there in the air; you don't *need* to buy them. If you're buying them from a lab, you're not embracing your terroir. You should just embrace what you have."

If you live in a town with a really good beer bar, you'll probably find something on tap with a bit of zing in it, something the brewery calls "wild." The next time you sample it, though, consider just how wild it actually is.

www.allaboutbeer.com, September 2015

POSTMODERN BEER

Joe Stange

From whence comes your beer, and does it matter to you? Does it affect how much you enjoy it?

For example: maybe you hold in your hand a pitch-perfect, West Coast-style imperial IPA — except it was made in Belgium. Or you're drinking a credible imitation of a Düsseldorf Altbier — except it was brewed in Vermont.

All beers come from somewhere. It's just that many of the beers we drink today are not especially connected to their own somewheres.

When made with technical know-how — because today's brewers can rebuild water chemistry, choose from a bewildering array of yeast strains, import all sorts of fresh ingredients, and adapt their process in seemingly infinite other ways — it seems that our beers could come from anywhere.

Consider an international beer firm like Mikkeller, which commissions a diverse range of products — many of them tasty, and virtually all technically excellent — from breweries in at least five countries. Maybe you've tasted the Mikkeller Texas Ranger, which is something like a chipotle chili porter, and thought something like, "Ah, so this is what Danish craft beer tastes like." But it was brewed in Lochristi, Belgium.

I call this postmodern beer, because it reminds me of things I learned in philosophy classes that I thought I would never, ever apply to real life. Hooray, college! Please hang in there as I try to walk that tricky line between not insulting your intelligence and boring the pants off, you know, everyone else.

Briefly: postmodernism cuts across all sorts of subjects and disciplines, many of them cultural. Its victims include art, architecture, music, literature and yes, food. The common theme is a detachment from location, or reality, or truth. The sign is detached from that which is signified; the map is less interested in the actual territory.

Hence we drink *Berliner weisse* — increasingly popular in the US — which has little or nothing to do with Berlin. It was brewed not in Berlin, and likely not in a way that old Berliner brewers would recognize. But it might taste good.

Meanwhile, in Berlin: what do most upstart brewers appear most interested in making? American-hopped ales. And so on.

It wasn't always like this — at least, not to this extent. I've only been drinking beer since the 1990s, but lately I've developed a fascination with beer books from the 1970s and '80s. They describe a simpler time, when each beer seemed to come from a place. People were just waking up to variety. That beer is clearly Belgian, that beer is clearly British, that beer is clearly German. The classic one is Michael Jackson's *World Guide to Beer* — I bought a used copy cheap online, and so can you. This influential book not only tells us about the beers, but it shows us the places in which they are drunk, the streets outside the cafés, the countryside around the breweries.

That book and many others showed us foreign beers from foreign places, and it was fascinating. It was exotic. But what does "foreign beer" even mean these days, when Beck's can be brewed in St Louis and Green Flash can be brewed in Hainaut?

We can suppose that in simpler times, most brewers had little choice in this — their beers would have had a sense of place whether they liked it or not. Their water was their water, their yeast was their yeast, and the most practical ingredients would have been the nearest ones. These and other decisions would have added up to a certain house character.

These days, brewers have infinite choices, but what's really interesting is that lately more of them appear to be choosing to pursue sense of place — they are trying to reconnect to their somewheres.

This is happening a lot with farmhouse ales, as brewers try to make more rustic old-fashioned beers, playing here and there with local microbiology.

A few examples:

Hoften Dormaal Saison in Tildonk, Belgium, is made in a real farm brewery using barley, wheat, spelt and hops that were all grown on the farm. An overnight cereal mash makes the unmalted wheat and spelt easier for the yeast to digest, but it's allowed to cool so that lactic bacteria can have their subtle say in the form of a light acidity.

Jester King Le Petit Prince is a table beer of 2.9%, fermented with a half-wild yeast blend collected from the air near Austin, Texas.

Bastogne Ardenne Saison, just south of the town of Bastogne, is first fermented with yeast from nearby Orval before getting a secondary dose of *brettanomyces* strains said to be harvested from local apples.

There are many more, and by now you can probably name a few. This is sense of place, not as an inevitability, but as a decision. A brewer can choose this path for all sorts of reasons: for ethics, because of concerns about the environment or local culture; for marketing, because it makes a good story that sells beer; or just for fun. Or all of the above.

As a drinker, my interests are hedonistic: I travel a lot, and if I think a beer says something about its home or its culture, I tend to enjoy it more. Beer is about pleasure, after all; for me the context is part of it.

It should be no surprise that philosophers have tried to grapple with what comes next. I reckon courses called "Beyond Postmodernism" have been around as long as postmodernism itself. Showing that great academic sense of imagination, many of them call it "post-postmodernism."

Yeah. We need a better name. But much of it shares a common theme: a return to reality. A return to place. A return to sincerity. Now: Do these beers represent sincere sincerity, or are they just fond imitations of simpler times?

I have no idea. But I look forward to tasting the attempts.

Draft, July 2015

A SENSE OF PLACE RETURNS

Stephen Beaumont

Back in the day, before jet travel between continents or winter tomatoes in snowy climes or "tickers" trading precious bottles of foreign brew through the mail, many beer styles had a distinct sense of place about them.

In many cases, this "terroir," if you will, had something to do with the regional brewing water. The original pilsners, for instance, so named because they were born in the Czech town of Pilsen, could attribute their gentle character at least in part to the softness of the local water. Classic British pale ale, on the other hand, boasts a firm, almost flinty maltiness thanks to the mineral-rich water of the Midlands brewing town of Burton-on-Trent, where the style was made famous.

Hops, too, tended to add locality to beer, as with the Bohemian Saaz hops in the aforementioned pilsner or Fuggles and Goldings in the archetypal British best bitter. Indeed, even today hops may play a role in the geography of beer, as with the role of the American-bred Cascade, Centennial and Citra hops — sometimes referred to collectively as the "C-hops" — in the stylistic off-shoots known as the American pale ale, or sometimes APA, and the various iterations of American style IPA, including black IPA, session IPA, white IPA and no doubt something newly developed since these words were set to print.

But thanks to the international hop trade, an American pale ale can today be brewed to authenticity in Milan or Melbourne, as easily as it can in Chico, California, or Yakima, Washington. And the ease with which brewers today may manipulate water profiles, adding or subtracting minerals as needed, means that Burton or Bohemian brewing water is attainable anywhere the proper equipment can be found.

So what is left for the role of "place" in beer? Surprisingly, quite a bit.

I reached this conclusion gradually over several years while visiting a series of what might best be called "new brewing lands," countries without long brewing histories, but where craft beer has nonetheless found a foothold, and nations where the global breweries had over decades virtually eliminated all beer styles other than golden lagers in varying degrees of lightness. And lands that may count themselves among both camps, such as Brazil.

My first inkling that "place" might have a role to play in the emerging Brazilian craft brewing scene came when I visited an early edition of the Festival Brasileiro da Cerveja, or Brazilian Beer Festival, in the southern town of Blumenau. It arrived in the form of a quartet of ales from Cervejaria Colorado, a pioneering Brazilian craft brewery since purchased by Anheuser-Busch InBev, each of which incorporated some sort of indigenous ingredient — coffee, honey, manioc (cassava starch) and a type of hard sugar known as *rapadura* — and a single strong lager from Cervejaria Way, aged on chips of an exotic wood more commonly used to age *cachaça*, called variously Amburana or Umburana.

More recently, I've watched as this local ingredient mantle has been taken up by other Brazilian brewers. Not being major growers of traditional brewing ingredients, but being blessed with the fruits — literal and figurative — of the Amazon basin, Brazilians have taken to brewing with fruits such as *bacuri* and *jabuticaba* — virtually untranslatable, but quite tasty — or employing any number of exotic woods in the aging of their beers. The results have often been most impressive and utterly without global equivalency.

Elsewhere in the Southern Hemisphere, Kiwi craft brewers have embraced the uniqueness of their local hops to create beer styles of their very own, New Zealand Pilsner and New Zealand Pale Ale chief among them. Respectively similar in structure to the Bohemian and American versions of those beer styles, the peculiar tropical fruitiness of New Zealand hops like Nelson Sauvin and Riwaka gives the Kiwi versions distinctive aromas and flavours otherwise unobtainable, while the deft hand of brewers acutely familiar with their local ingredients results in beers that are balanced and nuanced rather than "one-trick ponies" which scream their hoppy pedigree. In neighbouring Australia, brewers are well on course do the same with home-grown varieties of their own, in particular the Galaxy hop. Other distinctly Aussie hop varieties are in development, with brewers already rushing to discover their secrets.

National ingredients and processes can even change over time, as seems to be the case in Italy. Not long after their young craft brewing movement took flight, early Italian craft brewers embraced the chestnut as their calling card to the beer world — chestnut beers even have their own judging category at the annual national beer competition — although it seems today that penchant may be fading. My experience at a more recent Birra dell'Anno competition revealed, however, that if *birre alla castagna* have indeed had their day in Italy, their role as cultural flagship is being assumed most adeptly by what Italian brewers are referring to, in English, as "Italian grape ales," beers made with the addition of grape must or lees.

Even the great beverage imitators of Japan, having made their distinctive and indelible mark on the world of whisky, are now finding their own way in brewing. Saké yeast and various strains of rice are the most common components, but not to be discounted are the indigenous variety of barley cultivated from a mere six seeds by the Kiuchi brewery and, of course, the potential inherent in the repatriation of Japanese hop varieties such as Sorachi Ace.

These are but a few of the most obvious examples of "place" playing a burgeoning role in brewing. There are many other, less widespread examples, as well: *molé* spices being used in Mexican Imperial stout; traditional Chinese medicine (TCM) herbs in Beijing pale ale; marzipan-inspired beer from Toledo, Spain; the *bière de blé noire* of northern France, made with blackened buckwheat; and more.

Why any of this matters, or should matter, is best understood when viewed through the prism of the global beer industry, a trade increasingly dominated by bankers rather than brewers. Because in a world where German beer (Beck's) is brewed in the United States, Japanese beer (Sapporo) is brewed in Canada and any number of craft beers brewed around the world in countries other than Belgium are marketed as "Belgian," a beer that shouts its pedigree through the only thing that really counts, its taste, is surely something to be cherished.

2016

IMAGINARY FRIENDS: THE BEERS THAT NEVER WERE

Randy Mosher

One of the great frustrations of researching beer history is not being able to actually taste the beers. You can try to brew up a facsimile, but the further back you go, the less certainty you have. Prior to about 1600, you sometimes have just a few words to go by. Earlier than 1750 or so, written recipes remain tantalizingly vague. And complete recipes of a more recent date may employ different terminology, hard-to-pin-down ingredients, or obscure procedures to a point where the modern-day brewer cannot be sure if his or her efforts are anything more than wishful brewing.

Even with all their uncertainty, attempts at recreation can teach us about the beers of the past. And an historic perspective can be useful when trying to dream up new and unusual beers to brew. Thinking about history without having to worry about whether it is correct or not can be a great big hogshead of fun. Sometimes you just want to brew, history be damned.

Take the example of Scotch ale. British brewing books, as early as the 17th century, heap tun-loads of scorn on smoked malts in beer, and this goes for Scottish brewers, too. But we American brewers are so taken with the lore and heady flavours of Scotch whisky that we *imagine* that peat-smoked malt must be a component of Scottish beer as well. If you go back in time this undoubtedly was true, but the creosote reek of peated malt has been absent from Scottish beer for centuries. But why not re-imagine things? And you know, a bit of peat-smoked malt does add complexity to a malty Scotch ale.

In history, just about everything has been tried at one

time or another, so just make it up. Somebody, somewhere probably brewed it. Your beer may be correct, but you will probably never learn the who, when or why of it.

Fantasizing can be a powerful tool. You can make up beers that *might* have been brewed at known times and places or you can take it a great deal further. Just imagine . . .

A monastery in Southern Indiana where they brewed a dubbel called Two-X, that was a strong version of the common beers once brewed in the Ohio Valley, but with a dab of molasses and sassafras added. A pawpaw tripel lightened with sorghum or maple syrup was a seasonal favourite.

A mythic civilization that you could picture as a cross between the lands of *Lord of the Rings* and a giant amusement park, kind of an "Elves gone Wild" culture. Popular tipples might have included an ultra-pale springtime beer made from wheat with a sizeable addition of quince juice, dosed with ginger and woodruff; a wood-aged old ale with caramelized honey and aromatized with black truffles; and a velvety, ink-black black barley wine seasoned with several types of flower blossoms, not all of which are legal at the present time.

A secret community of brewers hidden in the Caliphate of 14th-century Baghdad. One beer was laced with thyme honey and seasoned with exotic spices such as saffron, jasmine, myrrh and coloured a burgundy red with Syrian rue (Google that one). A stupefying and very sweet barley wine was made with a number of additions of date or sometimes grape syrup, seasoned with cardamom. It was served with a small disk of gold leaf floating on top of the foam.

A beer-brewing offshoot of the Maya, somewhere in Honduras. A beer reserved for royalty used malted corn and native honey for the base, with cocoa beans, toasted hot *chiles*, vanilla pods and the pulp of the black sapote fruit, along with a whole kit of native herbs and vine barks that have been lost to time. Texture was heavy and sweet, bittered by the herbs and chocolate, enlivened by the brisk heat of the *chiles*.

A British expatriate village in the Oporto region of Portugal — famous for port wines — hanging on until the late nineteenth century. These crafty brewers made barley wines that were fortified with brandy distilled from honey wine and aged exactly like port, in retired port barrels. The everyday version was a wispy blonde, limpid and dry as a Fino Sherry, but with an unmistakable malty nose. A dark, sweet, extra luxurious ale was made with the addition of caramelized raisins and liquorice. It was said to be much improved by a shipboard journey to the New World and back.

A secret order of brewer-knights in France, who made off with brewing secrets from the ancient Middle East. Brewing in a regular seasonal progression for secret ceremonies and private meetings, these descendants of Crusaders kept alive a tradition of the legendary beers of the ancient world until about 1800. Egyptian Red Beer of Sekhmet, Babylonian Strong Emmer and Date Beer, Sumerian Blackened Raisin Ale and Yellow Soma Ale were among the most memorable.

A tiny town up near the Swiss border that somehow escaped the attention of Michael Jackson, still brewing gruit beers, although now using lager yeast. This manifests itself in a full range of beers, including a "Gruilsner", which is a pale lager, slightly stronger that a regular pale lager at 1055/13.6 °P, and seasoned primarily with bog myrtle (*myrica gale*), having decided that the astringent taste of yarrow and wild rosemary didn't suit the modern palate. Hops are used, but only in small amounts for preservative qualities. Breweries serve a "keller" version — dry-bog-myrtled, directly from the wood. The bock is the showcase for the gruit character and, in addition to the *myrica*, features caraway, long pepper (*piper longam*) and a dash each of sweet flag (*acorus calamus*) and mace.

An amber-coloured rye doppelbock that leaned heavily on the local Alpine juniper used to be popular around Christmastime.

This kind of fantasizing is not only a lot of fun, it is a really good way to stretch your imagination and break yourself free of your usual patterns. And when you go back to brew a pale ale, well, you know it's going to be a pretty interesting pale ale.

So we will part with just a few lingering questions, to which I will leave to you to invent the answers:

What might the Vikings and the Native Americans they ran into in Martha's Vineyard have brewed?

What will be the first beer brewed on Mars?

What would Elvis have brewed if he were an ardent homebrewer?

All About Beer, 2007

THE CRAFT BEER MANIFESTO

Simon Johnson

1. Only use distilled otter's tears
2. Use only barley that's been warmed by the breath of kindly owls
3. Craft beer cares, so only use hops that have been flown halfway around the world
4. You can have it any colour you like, as long as it's not brown. Unless it's an Indian Brown Ale
5. Beards allowed only if they're ironic
6. It's not "inconsistent", it's "experimental"
7. It's not "hiding faults", it's "barrel-ageing"

8. It's not "gone off", it's "challenging preconceptions of sour beer"
9. Ensure that the branding costs more than the brewhouse
10. Collaborate every month with an international brewer, a blogger, a celebrity and a musician
11. There are only seven ingredients in Craft Beer: hops, malt, water, yeast, YouTube, Twitter and Facebook
12. Our over-riding mantra - Craft Beer Is AWESOME!!!

www.reluctantscooper.blogspot.co.uk, February 2012

5

BEER JOURNEYS

Let a man walk ten miles steadily on a hot summer's day
along a dusty English road, and he will soon discover
why beer was invented.

G.K. Chesterton

A BAVARIAN TAVERN

Patrick Leigh Fermor

I strayed by mistake into a room full of SS officers, *Gruppen-* and *Sturmbannführers*, black from their lightning-flash-collars to the forest of tall boots underneath the table. The window embrasure was piled high with their skull-and-crossbones caps. I still hadn't found the part of this Bastille I was seeking, but at last a noise like the rush of a river guided me downstairs again to my journey's end.

The vaults of the great chamber faded in infinity through blue strata of smoke. Hobnails grated, mugs clashed and the combined smell of beer and bodies and old clothes and farmyards sprang at the newcomer. I squeezed in at a table full of peasants, and was soon lifting one of those *Masskrugs* to my lips. It was heavier than a brace of iron dumb-bells, but the blond beer inside was cool and marvellous, a brooding cylindrical litre of Teutonic myth. This was the fuel that had turned the berserk feeders upstairs into Zeppelins and floated them so far from heart's desire. The gunmetal-coloured cylinders were stamped with a blue HB conjoined under the Bavarian crown, like the foundry-mark on cannon. The tables, in my mind's eye, were becoming batteries where each gunner served a silent and recoil-less piece of ordnance which, trained on himself, pounded away in steady siege. *Mass*-gunfire! Here and there on the tables, with their heads in puddles of beer, isolated bombardiers had been mown down in their emplacements. The vaults reverberated with the thunder of a creeping barrage. There must have been over a thousand pieces engaged! – Big Berthas, Krupp's pale brood, battery on battery crashing at random or in salvoes as hands adjusted the elevation

159

and traverse and then tightened on the stone trigger-guard. Supported by comrades, the walking wounded reeled through the battle smoke and a fresh gunner leaped into each place as it fell empty.

My own gun had fired its last shot, and I wanted to change to a darker-hued explosive. A new *Mass* was soon banged down on the board. In harmony with its colour, it struck a darker note at once, a long Wagnerian chord of black-letter semibreves: *Nacht und Nebel!* Rolling Bavarian acres formed in the inscape of the mind, fanning out in vistas of poles planted pyramidally with the hops gadding over them heavy with poppy-sombre flowers.

A Time of Gifts, 1977

TWO NIGHTS AT THE BUD LIGHT HOTEL

John Holl

LAS VEGAS – The email that I received prior to my arrival in Sin City was specific. Representatives in blue-logoed polo shirts and black pants would be waiting by door 51 at Terminal C. They would escort me to the bus that would take me to the Hard Rock Hotel & Casino – dubbed for this week only as the Bud Light Hotel. I was surprised as the shuttle bus passed by the iconic multi-story tall neon guitar that is the icon of the hotel, the same one famously smashed in the climactic scene of the cinematic tour-de-force that is Nicholas Cage's *Con Air*. Personally, I was expecting a multi-story Bud Light bottle.

I won't often write in first person, but given that a hotel stay is a personal experience to the guest, I hope you will forgive this temporary break from form. As someone that regularly covers the beer industry, staying in what was essentially a commercial for two nights was a surreal experience.

Bud Light as a brand is a marketing force to be reckoned with. In recent years Anheuser-Busch InBev, the Belgian company that owns the brand, has been smart to attach it to promotions, events and artists that it believes will enhance its cache. Despite sales dropping 1.3 percent last year, according to Symphony IRI, a firm that monitors the industry, Bud Light is still rolling out millions of barrels of beer per year.

One such marketing tactic that keeps the brand in the public eye is this hotel concept. For the last several years Bud Light hotels have been popping up around the country tagged to specific events, like the National Nightclub & Bar Show (part of the reason I was recently in Las Vegas) as well as the Super Bowl. It was held in New Jersey this year, and the brand rented out a 4,000-passenger Norwegian cruise ship, docked it on the New York side of the Hudson River, and held a multi-day party for guests and visitors. The hotel concept made its first appearance in 2010, according to an emailed statement from Rob McCarthy, Vice President for Bud Light at Anheuser-Busch.

So there I was in Sin City, walking through a side entrance under the blue neon Bud Light Hotel sign, past the doors branded with the same logo, into a hospitality room thumping with dance music, complete with an indoor basketball hoop, a bar made of ice, and plenty of young women in very short shorts and very tight tank tops, also emblazoned with the Bud Light logo.

At check-in I was presented with a backpack with the logo pressed on, and various other logoed items, including a bottle coozie. Upon entering the room the branding deepened. The do-not-disturb card was emblazoned with Bud Light, as was the soap, the bottles of shampoo, and the room service menu (although judging by dusty layer on the $6 bag of potato chips resting on the dresser, there isn't much in-room noshing taking place at the Hard Rock).

Because the logo was everywhere I turned, I was genuinely confused that the one thing that I would expect a beer brand to offer — a logoed bottle opener — was simply a generic metal one (made in China, according to the sticker), the type that's generally found in a plastic fishbowl at the checkout counter of a liquor store.

Curious as well were the bottles of Bud Light in the mini-fridge. It's a beer best enjoyed fresh — it has about a four-month shelf life according to a brewer with the company — and the ones in my fridge were at the three-month mark. Not stale by any means, but certainly not super fresh.

So, back down to the hospitality room I went, where just-packaged 16-ounce aluminum bottle-shaped cans with twist off caps (eliminating the need for bottle openers) were offered from behind a bar made of ice. When I walked in, one of the gentlemen dressed in khakis and a black polo-shirt was jokingly calling out "Coors Light!" I raised an eyebrow as he passed me a Bud Light, and got the response, "No one can tell the difference."

The room was filled with the young women in their tight, revealing Bud Light uniforms, happily shooting hoops or dancing. On at least one evening the uniform was traded for white dresses. The men remained in khakis and polo shirts, or grey T-shirts.

"We typically hire temporary staff for events like Bud Light Hotel based on personality and fit with the brand image," said McCarthy. "In other words, we prefer to hire co-ed staffers who are fun, social, and are demographically consistent with our primary target of millennials." McCarthy says the Bud Light Hotel is "designed to be the ultimate fusion of sports and music, and its goal is to be the entertainment destination at the events where it's staged".

It's all of that for sure. It's also a testament to what money can buy. However, in covering this industry for a decade now I've come to know beer as personal to its drinkers, and that people are very loyal to their preferred brands. Bud Light is no exception, and I met people everywhere who were clearly tickled about staying at the hotel, for the experience of personally connecting with a brand they usually see on television or in their refrigerator.

Same for the Anheuser-Busch employees staying at the hotel. They are loyal to their company and their brands. They wear it on their sleeves, and are a good reminder that behind every multi-national corporation there are men and women who care, and work hard. I admire that a great deal.

It's a stunt, sure, but the guest interaction helped humanize a brand that can sometimes — at least from a media standpoint — be as cold as the suggested serving temperature.

"We want visitors to have a great time, and to feel like staying at Bud Light Hotel was a truly unforgettable experience," wrote McCarthy.

Well, mission accomplished.

All About Beer, April 2014

BEER IN GREECE

Professor X. Landerer

"*Tempora mutantur et homines in illis*", says an old Latin proverb: times change and men change with them. Fifty years ago there was in Nauplia a lone German brewer, who brewed beer for foreigners, Frenchmen, Germans, and Englishmen, who were the only consumers of this national beverage. The Greeks regarded him as a poisoner, *farmakia* in their language, and his wares were *farmaki*, or poison, on account of their bitterness. Now, beer is the popular beverage, ranking side by side with champagne on the bill of fare, in all the hotels. If the populace want a treat, they go to the beer house.

All beers brewed in Athens, and there are some exceedingly good strong kinds produced, are rich in all the nutritives cereals contain. Among the brewers is a German, Bachauer, whose beer is recognised as the best. The necessary malt is imported from Austria and Bavaraia, Greek barley being ill adapted for malting; the hops also are brought from Germany. Wild hops are found in the mountains, especially in Macedonia; they are picked by the monks, sent to the brewers and sold. The brewers who settled in Athens made many attempts to cultivate hops. The plants flourished well, but they were no hop-growers, and it is a pity hop growing did not receive better attention.

All kinds of beer, no matter how expensive it may be, is drunk and prized, especially by the public, if it only foams well, even if somewhat sour, as long as it does not take the edge off the teeth. Brewers are still free agents here, for there are no strict investigations into the value of the beverage, consequently every brewer — there are only six large enough to be worth mention in Athens — and every beer-seller, of which there are about twenty — brews how he chooses, and it is all consumed, for beer drinking has extended through all Greece, even into the newest sections of Greece and Epirus, and beer has become fashionable everywhere. In the seaport towns beer of every other national make is to be obtained, particularly English beer, and all these beers, good and bad, find sale at a high price and are drunk. Consequently there is an excellent prospect for brewers to do a good business in the East by establishing, according to the nature of the locality, large or small breweries.

As an epilogue to these lines, we may add that beer, styled *zitos*, was known in the oldest times. In Egypt, Osiris is supposed to have introduced it as a substitute for wine and other spirituous drinks. To the ancient Hellenes this drink was not unknown, and Aeschinos and Sophocles make mention of *krithinos inos – inos krithys*, i.e. barley wine. Xenophon's soldiers drank barley wine on their retreat, and in order to preserve it from souring, buried it in the earth in huge stone vessels called *pitharia*. The word beer, according to my opinion, is derived from the old English *bere*, of a brown colour; or from the verb to brew, i.e. a long boiling of any substance. *Ger. And Amer. Brewer's Journal.*

Country Brewer's Gazette, 23 April 1884

WELSH ALE

George Borrow

"I suppose you get your ale from Llangollen," said I, "which is celebrated for its ale over Wales."

"Get our ale from Llangollen?" said Tom, with a sneer of contempt, "no, nor anything else. As for the ale, it was brewed in this house by your honour's humble servant."

"Oh," said I, "if you brewed it, it must of course be good. Pray bring me some immediately, for I am anxious to drink ale of your brewing."

"Your honour shall be obeyed," said Tom, and disappearing returned in a twinkling with a tray on which stood a jug filled with liquor and a glass. He forthwith filled the glass, and pointing to its contents said: "There, your honour, did you ever see such ale? Observe its colour! Does it not look for all the world as pale and delicate as cowslip wine?"

"I wish it may not taste like cowslip wine," said I; "to tell you the truth, I am no particular admirer of ale that looks pale and delicate; for I always think there is no strength in it."

"Taste it, your honour," said Tom, "and tell me if you ever tasted such ale."

I tasted it, and then took a copious draught. The ale was indeed admirable, equal to the best that I had ever before drunk — rich and mellow, with scarcely any smack of the hop in it, and though so pale and delicate to the eye nearly as strong as brandy. I commended it highly to the worthy Jenkins, who exultingly exclaimed: "That Llangollen ale indeed! No, no! Ale like that, your honour, was never brewed in that trumpery hole Llangollen."

Wild Wales, 1862

Anti-Freeze For The World's Frozen Wastes

Brian Glover

Beer seems to be sliding down the thermometer. Once a glass was served at cellar temperature. Now it's cool to expect it straight out of the deep freeze.

Once you asked for Guinness. Now you have the "choice" of the standard drop or extra cold at 2.5C° cooler. Soon bar staff will ask if you want ice — that's if there isn't already a frozen head of snow on the top. But in the deep midwinters of the past, beer was not just a chilly draught. Some were expected to warm you. They were more antifreeze than frozen waste. And none were better at providing essential heating than brews designed for the purpose.

Simonds of Reading used to brew a bottle of Archangel Stout which claimed to be "specifically brewed for the Arctic". It was certainly "X"-certificate stuff, with seven Xs on the label, compared to five on the brewery's Old Berkshire Strong Ale. The label showed sailing ships struggling through ice floes, on the way to the Russian port of Archangel. This brew was Simonds' answer to Barclay's Russian Imperial Stout. It was not a cheap option in the pub. A tiny nip bottle would set you back 1s 4d in 1951, compared to 8d for a half-pint bottle of brown ale or a shilling for a pint of mild. It was more aimed at the shoppers in Harrods, for whom Simonds also bottled a strong ale, than the public bar boozer.

Archangel Stout was a short-lived occasional brew. It was not introduced until after the Second World War, when the British convoys to Archangel had been famous for supplying the Soviet Union. Once Simonds merged with Courage and Barclay in 1960, it sank into history. But another beer has a longer and more authentic Arctic tale.

Allsopp's Arctic Ale was first brewed more than 150 years ago in 1851 — and it really was specifically brewed for the Arctic.

For centuries men had dream about finding a sea route round North America — the legendary North-West passage — to provide a much shorter path to the Far East than stormy Cape Horn. Men like Hudson, Cabot and Chancellor tried to discover it — and failed. Some died in the attempt. In 1845 Sir John Franklin set off on another search, and was never seen alive again. Six years later, the Government decided to send Admiral Belcher to find him. Burton brewer Samuel Allsopp was asked to produce a beer "suitable for the rigours of the Arctic climate'.

It was so strong, it was claimed that the thick wort would not run from the copper through the tap in the normal way, but had to be "lifted out with buckets". Its colour was a rich ruby brown and it was said to taste like old Madeira.

Allsopp's Arctic Ale was launched at the Royal Harwich Yacht Club in 1852, from where the expedition set out, and proved a great success with the frostbitten crew. Belcher later reported: "It has indeed been a great blessing for us, particularly for our sick. It kept exceedingly well and was sought after by all." Despite its high alcohol content, it did partially freeze, forcing out the bottle stoppers. But once the "semi-frozen spongy mass" had been re-bottled and thawed out, it proved just as good as ever. A polar star was born.

But while the ale was a success, the expedition was not. It was not until another voyage in 1857, also fuelled with Arctic Ale, that Franklin's frozen remains were found by Sir Leopold McLintock. From then on, no polar expedition was complete without a cargo of crates. It also proved popular in some surprising foreign markets, notably the West Indies. But at home, it seemed to be too heavy and sweet for most tastes.

After Allsopp merged with its Burton neighbour in 1934, Ind Coope tried to boost sales in the 1950s with full-page magazine adverts for the beer which "keeps out the cold". Arctic Ale was also sold as a Christmas six-pack, with leaflets giving recipes for Arctic pudding and a beer punch.

But once Ind Coope was swallowed inside the Allied Breweries giant in 1961, the niche beer's days were numbered. Allied decided Arctic Ale was "untrendy" and in 1970 replaced it with a lighter, drier brew, Triple A.

Arctic Ale had hit its final iceberg, but there is still one reminder of British beer's links with the Polar Regions written into every atlas today. It comes from a London brewery once more famous than Fuller's and Young's combined. It stood on the banks of the River Thames, just up river from Fuller's at Brentford.

One of the oldest breweries in Britain, the Red Lion Brewery on Brentford High Street was by the early 19th century owned by Felix Booth, who also ran a nearby distillery noted for Booth's gin.

In 1829 Booth agreed to fund an expedition by his friend John Ross in 1829 in search of the North-West Passage. It cost him the then considerable sum of £17,000 — but it was well worth it. After a visit by William IV to the brewery in 1832, the grateful king granted the brewery a royal warrant. Its name was changed to the Royal Brewery and the Royal coat of arms was proudly hung above the entrance.

Of more lasting significance, in recognition of his benefactor, Ross named the most northern peninsula of the American mainland Boothia. It's still there on the map, north of Hudson Bay. The Royal Brewery was not so enduring: it was beheaded by a takeover. In 1922 the firm was seized by Style & Winch of Maidstone in Kent, and closed the following year. An early pioneer of improved public houses, the Royal's cause was probably not helped by its slogan, "Sensible Houses for Sensible Men". No doubt the company regarded pubs that sold its potent Arctic Ale as silly houses for insensible men.

Beer, January 2004

MY TWO ROUNDS OF A FRIENDLY
GERMAN BEER BOUT

Will Hawkes

12 March 2015 — It's lunchtime in Düsseldorf, and at Füchschen, one of the city's great old-town breweries, the discussion has turned to beer. In particular, Kölsch, the traditional beer of Cologne, Düsseldorf's great rival.

"If you want my honest opinion, it's something you can chug," says Frank Driewer, head brewer. "It's something you can drink after you have mown your lawn. It's refreshing." I'm not certain — Driewer has an impressive poker face — but I think I can detect the hint of a smirk. "Refreshing" is not a compliment in the minds of beer aficionados.

It's telling, that smile. I'm in Germany to find out just how serious the rivalry between Düsseldorf and Cologne is. (And it was fortunate timing: At the time, the euro was tumbling against the value of the dollar, which ended at its highest value against the common European currency in 12 years on Wednesday.)

Even before my encounter with Driewer — before I arrive in Germany, to tell the truth — I'm far from convinced. People say these two cities, united by the wide, muddy-blue Rhine, are fierce opponents, divided by competing Carnivals, sports, money, politics and beer. But how intense could this animosity be?

It's beer that particularly interests me. The cities drink different drops; while Cologne has the delicate, perfumed, pale Kölsch, Düsseldorf has Alt, a dark-copper, bitter, extremely drinkable brew. What's more, in a land famed for its bottom-fermented lagers, they're both top-fermented, the same as pale ales and stouts. Perhaps, I think, as my train pulls into Cologne's central station, that similarity is the first hint that this is a rivalry that's more friendly than fratricidal.

I head for Brauhaus Sion, a huge, rambling beer hall in Cologne's Old Town. It's noon and the place is slowly filling up. It's time for my first lesson in Cologne tradition: my beer comes in a cylindrical 200-millilitre glass (just less than half a standard US pint), and it is delivered to my table by a blue-clad Köbes, the traditional Rhineland waiter, whose gruffness is apparently part of the fun.

That's not all. To my left is a glass display case containing three grinning male mannequins, all of them in extravagant Carnival costumes. One has pigtails, another wears an exuberant ruff and the third, nearest to me, is sporting a headdress made from peacock feathers.

As I marvel at the intricacy of these remarkable outfits, the Köbes dumps a plate of blood sausage, mashed potato and stewed apples in front of me. This is *Himmel und Äad* (Heaven and Earth), a traditional Rhineland meal. It's an uncompromising dish; soft and heavy, salty and sweet — and not, in all honesty, particularly delicious.

Still, at least I'm full; I'll need the energy. I stumble out into bright winter sunlight and walk toward the 13th-century, twin-spired cathedral. It's a magnificent, humbling space, full of ancient interest, but my attention is drawn to the playful, elegant multi-coloured checkerboard stained-glass windows at the southern end, created by German artist Gerhard Richter in 2006.

I exit — avoiding a stout, flute-playing man whose comical jig has drawn a small crowd, if not much cash — and wander across to the Romano-Germanic Museum. Inside, there's an echo of that window in the patterned mosaics, the most impressive being the famous 3rd-century Dionysus Mosaic, which depicts cavorting maenads and satyrs attending to the Greek god of wine.

The message is clear: Cologne has a long and remarkable history — although you wouldn't know it from much of the Old Town, which was bombed heavily in the Second World War. I walk down Hohe Strasse, a shopping street. It's lively, to say the least. A TV crew is interviewing shoppers — Cologne is Germany's media capital — and a hole-in-the-wall place that sells fries, complete with ketchup, mayonnaise or curry mayonnaise, is doing a busy trade.

I drop in here and there for a glass of Kölsch. I'm getting to know the different beers — or, at least, that's what I fondly imagine. Sion is unremarkable; Früh has a lasting, enjoyably juicy malt character; Päffgen is soft and bitter and in my view the best of the trio. I find the last at its brewhouse on Friesenstrasse — where the beer is dispensed from small oak barrels in the corridor — and then, in the evening, at Gaststätte Lommerzheim, on the other side of the Rhine, which is full to bursting at 6 p.m. I am, too, after a few glasses of beer and a pork chop the size of Switzerland.

I'm keen to get an expert's view of Cologne culture, so the next morning I meet Michael Euler-Schmidt, deputy director of the Kölnishes Stadtmuseum and director of a group that promotes Cologne culture. He tells me that both Carnival and Kölsch are linked to the same traditions of sociability and democracy. "The people of Cologne love human contact," he says. "They are easy-going, they love to entertain, they are sociable. A Cologne pub is very democratic."

That afternoon, after a stroll around the museum (which boasts an exhibit on Kölsch, naturally) and lunch in the cavernous Gaffel am Dom, I decide to leave the Old Town. I walk down Schildergasse, reputedly the busiest shopping street in Europe, and across Neumarkt. Out here the streets are quieter and wider: There are kiosks on each corner selling, among other things, Kölsch, and even in this cold, a few hardy souls are drinking in the open.

But I have an appointment at Hellers Brauhaus. Compared with the names in the Old Town, Hellers are new boys, having been here only since 1991. They're more expansive than their rivals, brewing a number of styles, including (since December 2013) Alt. Nonetheless, as owner Anna Heller tells me, 70 per cent of the beer sold at Hellers is Kölsch. "We are very tolerant in Cologne, except about beer," she tells me, smiling. "When we first made the Alt, we got some letters. They were not nice."

She dates this resistance to the Kölsch Convention of 1986, which states Kölsch must be brewed only in Cologne (it's now part of European law). It's an interesting document, not least because Kölsch's history only dates to the early years of the 20th century. Alt (it means old) has a much longer history, but no restrictions on where it can be brewed.

My final stop of the day is Haus Töller, a classic Cologne pub, where I eat and drink a little more Päffgen. As I get up to leave, my coat brushes the table behind me and I hear the crash of a Kölsch glass hitting the floor. The manager smiles and waves away my concern; "It wouldn't be a proper night in here if at least one glass didn't get smashed," he says.

The next morning I'm on the train to Düsseldorf, a 30-minute ride north. It's not long before I'm at my first stop, Füchschen, and that encounter with brewmaster Peter Driewer. It's Wednesday lunchtime, and every table in the main restaurant, with rustic decor similar to decor in places I visited in Cologne, is taken. Charming little mustard pots sit on the tables: This city is famous for its mustard as well as its beer. I admit that my first sip of alt (bitter, full-bodied, caramel-rich) is a wonderful relief after the relative uniformity of Kölsch.

After lunch I scout Old Town, which retains more pre-war character than Cologne's. This is a wealthy place: The pubs and restaurants do a roaring trade, there are art galleries galore and the shopping street Königsallee is all luxury brands. (Even if Cologne has the busiest, Düsseldorf surely has the richest.)

It's a bit rich for my tastes, and anyway, it's really cold out. It's time for another Alt, this time from Uerige, whose idiosyncratic brewhouse can be found on Berger Strasse, right in the heart of the Old Town. I sit in the corridor and, eventually, a Köbes brings me a glass. It's one of the most remarkable beers I've ever had. Extraordinarily bitter by German standards, there's something about it that I can't quite put my finger on. It doesn't matter. It's delicious.

I sit and watch life go by. Two waiters stand and chat, hands on hips, gazing at the ceiling; another offers Mettbrötchen — a sort of pork tartare on bread — from a tray. It's an amazing place, but the Alt in front of me demands my attention; the bitterness grows and grows. Unlike Kölsch, which acts as an elegant but understated social lubricant, Alt refuses to be ignored.

Düsseldorf's past does not come close to Cologne's, however. While the latter can trace its history back to the Romans, Düsseldorf's rise came only with industrialization in the 19th century (giving the lie to a claim that the rivalry with Cologne started with the Battle of Worringen in 1288). At the Stadtmuseum — the city museum — I discover that the city grew from 14,000 inhabitants in 1816 to 328,000 in 1914. (I'm also charmed to learn that when Carnival restarted here after the Second World War, it did so with the cry: "Hooray! We are still alive!")

The key moment came, though, at the end of that conflict, when Düsseldorf was named capital of North Rhine-Westphalia, the region that includes Cologne. Perhaps that explains, at least partly, Düsseldorf's bullishness — and Cologne's passion for its own past.

In the early evening I join Altbier Safari, a popular tour of the Old Town's four breweries, plus nearby Im Goldenen

Kessel, where we taste Schumacher, a spicy, fruity, less robust brew than Füchschen or Uerige. Tour leader and company owner Eberhard Fischer, who used to work for a Cologne brewery, insists that Düsseldorfers are less hung up about beer. "People in Düsseldorf are more relaxed," he tells me. "If you want to buy a Kölsch here, it's not a problem."

The next morning I wander down to the Rheinturm, a 790-foot-high tower to the south of the Old Town, from which Cologne Cathedral can be seen. Or, at least, it can on a clear day. After the rapid elevator ascent, I'm slightly disappointed. Much is shrouded in low clouds, but the view of the mighty Rhine is impressive.

I'm short on time, so I descend and head for Immermannstrasse, where the signs are in two languages: German and Japanese. Düsseldorf has had one of Europe's largest Japanese populations since after the war. I choose the restaurant Takumi for lunch, where a bowl of rich, umami-heavy pork ramen is just the thing after four days of German food.

There's time for a few final glasses of Alt. I retrace my steps to Füchschen, where the gentle bonhomie in the bar reminds me of a moment during my chat with Driewer a day earlier. Brewing staff are not supposed to roll barrels through the pub, but one had, and straight past his boss, too. "That's Rhineland," said Driewer, laughing.

That relaxed spirit, I decide as I drain my last alt, is common to Cologne and Düsseldorf. The beers might be different, Düsseldorf might be wealthier and more multinational, Cologne a touch livelier and certainly more historic, but these are cities with more in common than most.

The rivalry is friendly. After all, why let petty squabbling spoil a good drink?

Washington Post, March 2015

BEER CONSUMPTION IN TURKEY

One of the most remarkable features of the German Consular Service is the care and accuracy with which reports upon trade in foreign countries are compiled, and then placed, through the medium of the Press, before the notice of business people who are likely to be interested. We venture to think that much of the success of Germany in competing with English exporters is due to the fact that the German Consuls are instructed from headquarters to ascertain not only what articles are needed, but the conditions under which transactions should be carried out.

As an example of a German Consular report, we refer our readers to one just issued by the German Consul-General at Constantinople, in which the consumption of beer in Turkey is dealt with. We do not propose to quote this report in detail, but the following abstract will be sufficiently significant and may possibly prove suggestive to brewers who cultivate export trade: -

The beer consumption of Turkey has increased enormously during the past few years, and at the present moment is increasing out of all proportion. Formerly the Turks did not drink beer, it being regarded as contrary to the Koran, in which beer is forbidden; but somehow or other the followers of Allah have managed to satisfy their consciences on this point, and the taste for beer has been rapidly acquired by the natives. Of course it is to the foreign element in Turkey that the introduction of beer is due, and the number of foreigners living in Turkey is increasing year by year, owing to restrictions upon residents having been largely removed. Nevertheless, we cannot look to the foreign residents for the great increase in the consumption of beer in Turkey; in is the natives who are responsible for it.

In Turkey, apparently, cask beer is most appreciated, though it is believed that the bottled beer trade will shortly assume large proportions. The greater part of this beer is imported via Austria-Hungary. However, there are breweries now existent in Turkey, and the following statistics, which have been compiled by the Greek Chamber of Commerce, are significant: –

	Local beers	Value, Turkish Pfd.
Brewery Bomonti	15,000 hl.	22,500
Other breweries	1,200	1,444
	Introduced beers	
Via Trieste per steamer	7,202	16,527
" Munich per rail	4,185	16,224
From Hungary	2,812	5,624
TOTAL	30,899	62,319

In Constantinople, therefore, beer to the value of M. 1,150,000, two-thirds draught and one-third bottled beer is consumed.

The report does not inform us as to the character of the local beer which is consumed in Turkey, but we shall hope to obtain some information on this subject before long. The report, however, is more explicit in regard to the foreign beers, which are most preferred. At first, German merchants endeavoured to create a taste for Pilsener, and taverns or bars were opened in various parts of Constantinople and well stocked with bottled Pilsener beers; but very little trade was done and these taverns, etc., were soon closed. Not to be daunted, the Germans then opened places where Munich beer became popular and is today greatly preferred. Clearly, the Turkish taste lies in the direction of the heavier rather than the lighter kinds of bottled beers, and consequently, if our own brewers determine to obtain a portion of Turkish custom they would do well to bar this fact in mind.

Bottled beer is very dear at Constantinople, and is beyond the reach of the working classes of the population; indeed, it is only the well-to-do who drink Munich beer. Barrelled beer is sold at 18-19 marks per hectolitre, or about 0.28 marks for a litre glass. A half-litre glass can be obtained for about 0.55 marks. There is evidently scope for the introduction of a moderately light beer which can be retailed at a price which will compete with that obtained at present by those who are selling Munich beer.

Brewers Journal, 15 May 1900

A Rising Tide Of Beer

Emile Zola

All round there was a rising tide of beer, widow Désir's barrels had all been broached, beer had rounded all paunches and was overflowing in all directions, from noses, eyes — and elsewhere. People were so blown out and higgledy-piggledy, that everybody's elbows or knees were sticking into his neighbour and everybody thought it great fun to feel his neighbour's elbows. All mouths were grinning from ear to ear in continuous laughter.

Germinal, 1885

THE NIGHT OF THE BIG WIND

Martyn Cornell

IPA, or India Pale Ale, as its name implies, was a beer designed originally for the Indian market: to be exact, the thousands of British-born "factors", or traders, and the "civil servants" and "military servants" employed by the mighty East India Company to look after and protect its enormous business interests on the sub-continent in the 18th and early 19th centuries. IPA was not a particularly strong beer for the time, but it was brewed with extra hops to ensure it survived the long four-month journey by sailing ship from Britain to Bombay, Madras or Calcutta, and it was enormously appreciated by men — and women — thousands of miles from home and eager for a taste of what they had left behind.

Extra-hopped pale ale was being exported to India from at least the 1740s, brewed at first in London and borne away by armed merchant ships called East Indiamen, which would carry a variety of European goods out to sweating expats, from foodstuffs to furniture, and return with cotton goods, spices, ivory and the like. From 1822 the brewers of Burton-upon-Trent, men such as Michael Bass, Samuel Allsopp and Thomas Salt, entered the market and began shipping out "pale ale as prepared for India". But this highly hopped beer had few or no sales at home in Britain — until, it appears, the aftermath of one of the worst storms ever to hit the British Isles.

In mid-December 1838, a 584-tonne East Indiaman called the *Crusader*, "a fine large ship with painted [gun] ports and a full-length figurehead", "newly coppered", that is, with new copper sheathing on the hull to prevent attacks by wood-boring molluscs, and "a very fast sailer", under the command of Captain J.G. Wickman, was getting ready to leave Liverpool for Bombay, with a cargo that included cases of glass shades, iron ingots, tin plates, beef and pork in casks, Government dispatches – and India ale in hogsheads, brewed by two different Burton brewers, Bass and Allsopp, the whole lot being insured for £100,000, perhaps £8 million today.

However, adverse winds seem to have kept increasing numbers of ships in Liverpool right through that Christmas and into the New Year. Finally, on Sunday, 6 January 1839, the wind changed, blowing a south-westerly breeze, and some 60 vessels, including the *Crusader*, left the Mersey. But what none of those sailors knew as they surged out into the Irish Sea was that a massive, fast-moving depression was coming in across the Atlantic, travelling from the west-south-west at around 40 to 50 knots, and bringing with it hurricane-force winds.

The storm, when it hit, battered towns and cities from the west coast of Ireland to the east coast of England, uprooted millions of trees, smashed down thousands of chimneys, sank hundreds of boats and killed several hundred people. In Ireland, where estimates have suggested between 200 and 400 people died, it became known as the "Night of the Big Wind". Thousands of houses and cottages were stripped of their roofs from Galway to Armagh. Limerick resembled "a city on which a park of artillery had played for a fortnight". In Belfast "not a roof escaped", while Dublin looked, according to one newspaper report, as if it had been sacked by an army, with houses burning or levelled to the ground, and "the rattling of engines, cries of firemen and labours of the military" presenting "the very aspect and mimicry of real war".

The winds seem to have struck the west coast of Britain late on the evening of Sunday 6th, and did not finally ease up until Tuesday morning. Nowhere from one side of the Pennines to the other was spared. In Liverpool, thousands spent a sleepless night listening to slates and bricks crashing down into the streets, as even "the best built houses rocked and shook" to the winds, and at least 20 people were killed by falling masonry. In Manchester, where six people died, so many factory chimneys were blown down, it was reckoned between 12,000 and 15,000 workers would be laid off for weeks before those chimneys could be rebuilt and the steam engines that powered the factories restarted. In Bolton, it was said, "not a house escaped", in Blackburn alone 11 factory chimneys were felled, and in Newcastle upon Tyne "almost every building suffered, more or less". In Ayr "the streets are covered with slates and chimney cans", and in Dumfries "the noise during the entire night was more deafening than the battle field". Birmingham and Wolverhampton had scarcely a street where houses had not suffered: much of the roof of Birmingham Town Hall was torn off, with lumps of lead weighing almost half a ton crashing into the street or onto nearby houses. Among the windmills demolished were five at Bridlington: others, such as the water company's windmill in Newcastle, were set on fire by the friction caused when the fierce winds set their sails rotating far faster than their builders had thought possible. In Barnsley the lead roof was lifted off the Methodist chapel and more factory chimneys demolished, while Leeds saw at least eight mill and factory chimneys levelled, and a church lose 24 feet off its spire. One remarkable phenomenon reported by the newspapers after the storm was a covering of what appeared to be sea salt on hedges, trees and houses in districts far inland, such as Huddersfield, more than 50 miles from the coast.

At sea the effects of the storm were terrifying and terrible, from the mouth of the Shannon to the mouth of the Humber. Many of the ships that had left Liverpool on the Sunday escaped the rage of the winds: but many others did not. Ships on their way home from ports far away, and close to the end of their journeys, were also caught. Between 30 and 40 vessels were either sunk or run aground in the Mersey area alone. Several went down with all their crews drowned. Those ships that ran onto sandbanks were then battered by the high winds and huge waves, and began to break up. Lifeboats could not get out to rescue the passengers and crews until the storm lessened, and when rescuers did arrive, they found many of those they were seeking to save had died of exposure in the preceding hours, on deck or in the rigging. The *Lockwood*, an emigrant ship bound for New York, which had got as far as Anglesey on the Sunday before being driven back by the storm, had then struck sandbanks and begun to list. Of the 110 passengers and crew, 53 died before rescuers could take them off. One of *Crusader*'s fellow East Indiamen, the *Brighton*, returning from Bombay, struck a sandbank in the mouth of the Mersey on the morning of Monday, 7 January and started breaking up. Some 14 of her crewmen made a raft and launched it into the mountainous waves to try to reach land. They were never seen again. The captain and his remaining crew had to cling to the rigging until Tuesday morning before the Liverpool lifeboat could come to their rescue.

What happened to the *Crusader* at sea appears to be unrecorded, but like other ships she was driven back by the violence of the storm, or, having failed to get past the tempest, tried unsuccessfully to return to the safety of port. On the morning of Tuesday, 8 January, nearly two days after she had left Liverpool, and after a "fearful night of wind, hail, thunder and sleet and forked lightning", the *Crusader* was seen just off the coast at Blackpool, more than 25 miles north of the Mersey. She had struck a sandbank that is still, today, named after her, Crusader Bank, and suffered "much damage". The ship's crew were firing the *Crusader's* guns to try to attract attention onshore, but soon after, according to the *Blackburn Standard* newspaper, "two boats put from her, and after crossing the breakers, landed a crew of 26 seamen, when a loud huzza proclaimed their safety."

According to one report, the crew had poured oil on the sea to calm the waves before they launched the boats

While the crew were safe, however, the ship had broken her back, and with her hull being almost covered by water at half-tide, her cargo began to wash ashore along a 15-mile stretch of coast from the Ribble in the south to the Wyre in the north. "A great deal" of the cargo, however, was gathered in by customs officers and locked up, including 79 hogsheads of ale that had been driven on shore, along with other goods, on 16 January (there was much cargo from other ships also washed up on the coast, along with dead bodies). The *Crusader* began properly to break up only on Sunday, 17 February, more than five weeks after she had run aground, though she fell to pieces within four days. However, the first sale of by the insurance underwriters of cargo saved from the wreck of the *Crusader* had already taken place, on Thursday, 7 February. It included cotton fabrics, woollen cloth, silk scarves and veils, tin plates — and "India ale, Bass and Alsop's [sic] brands".

Another two sales of goods saved from the wreck of the *Crusader*, including more India ale, took place in Liverpool on 14 March and 28 March. Three decades later, in 1870, a former employee of the shipping company that was sending the beer out east declared that this was the incident that first brought India Pale Ale to wide public notice in Britain. Pale ale was "very little known in London, except to those engaged in the India trade," he said. But when casks of salvaged IPA were put up for auction after the wreck of the *Crusader*, "an enterprising publican or restaurant keeper in Liverpool purchased a portion of the beer and introduced it to his customers; the novelty pleased, and, I believe, laid the foundation of the home trade now so extensively carried on."

Although IPA was known of in Liverpool before the wreck of the *Crusader* — the first use of the expression East India Pale Ale in a British publication actually comes from a Liverpool newspaper, in 1835, in an advertisement by the London brewer Hodgson's, directed at "merchants and private families" — the surge in popularity for the beer in Britain seems to have happened in the couple of years after 1839. In 1841 sales were going well enough in the city for Bass to open a store in Liverpool for the sale of "pale India ale", where "a Stock is kept of an age suitable for immediate consumption", while the brewer boasted, with some exaggeration: "This ale, so long celebrated in India, has now become an article of such great consumption in this country (where it is almost superseding every other sort of malt liquor)." There was also a considerable jump that year in adverts for IPA in London newspapers, though this seems to be more to do with the opening of a railway line between Burton-upon-Trent and London, which allowed that town's brewers to get their beer to the capital in hours rather than the weeks it had previously taken by canal. But in the North, it appears, we must thank the Big Wind for bringing IPA to drinkers' attentions.

www.zythophile.co.uk, October 2015

CHRISTMAS EVE IN MALAWI

Paul Theroux

He stopped walking. He wiped his face with a bunched hanky and read, DRINK LION — YOU WILL INJOY. Under that sign slumped a larger-than-usual native hut which gave the appearance of being supported by some six or seven Africans who leaned against it for shade. Their heads were stuck under the eaves of the overhanging brooms of roof thatch. In front there was a smaller but more professional sign, GUINNESS FOR POWER – BIG DRUM BAR, bearing the motif of a black fist punching jagged cartoon lightning; a small scrawl on a pasted label warned, *No Hawking*.

Ropes of hanging beads were strung over the doorway. Calvin pushed through them, dropping his creaking suitcase and, after ordering a beer, fanned himself with his hat – once a fairly good panama, now a wreck, with grubby crown and bitten brim (it was turned down front and back like a spy's, but very dirty). The bar was dark. When Calvin's eyes grew accustomed to the deep gloom he saw a row of Africans staring at him. Ragged and with unsteady heads, the Africans squatted on the dirt floor. They had wide machetes across their knees; each man balanced a pint of Lion on his knifeblade. Calvin smiled at them. They nodded back dark hellos.

Strangely, there was no picture of Dr Osbong in the bar. He was the President of Malawi. It was against the law not to have his picture in a conspicuous place in every building in the country. Calvin had one in his office. There had been one in the bar; a nail and a rectangle of cobwebs remained. Calvin did not mention its absence; it was none of his business.

The bar floor gave off a ripe stable-smell and was spread with looping rosaries of black ants. Almost immediately some ants located Calvin's suitcase. They swarmed into the mesh of the raffia, violating the contents. Calvin put his hat down. Leaning on the counter's sticky rings, one fist pressed into his cheek to aim his head at the ants, he gazed with that fatigued curiosity of strangers to hot climates. He was gasping for breath, trickles of sweat were running down the sides of his face, meeting at his chin and dripping onto his smudged shirtfront. A drop of sweat made its way like an insect down his breastbone to nest in his navel.

The temperature was in the mid-eighties, but there was no sun: it had risen and once off the ground disappeared into shapeless grey haze. A dull sky made the day throb with sunless heat, a kind of cookery worse than sunshine. The steamy air was a sickness; there was no fan in the bar, no electricity in the dorp.

A dusty bottle of beer was brought and opened, so warm it spewed suds. The bartender — wearing a paper party-hat with a sweat-diluted Lion slogan on it — slipped a soda straw into the bottle.

"A glass, please."

"No want straw?"

Straws were favoured, especially for drinking beer. Osbong said Malawi could take credit for the invention of the straw; in olden times it was a reed from a marsh, and still in the villages the common beer-pot was drunk out of by a circle of men with four-foot reed straws. "He spits through his straw" was a local proverb. The row of squatting blacks sucking on straws, balancing their pints on their knives, lifted their eyes to Calvin.

"No want," said Calvin. Straws gave him gas.

The bartender lifted out the straw and emptied it of beer by blowing through it hard. He replaced it in the cardboard box. Pouring Calvin a glass of beer he said, "Happy Christmas, bwana."

"Somehow," said Calvin, "it doesn't feel like Christmas. No offence intended."

Propped on the counter a new ad from the Lion breweries showed a comical lion in a red stocking hat and white St Nick whiskers; the ad was edged in plastic holly. A small tinsel Christmas tree dangled from a twist of yellow fly-paper in the centre of the room. Dabs of cotton-wool had been carefully glued onto the smeared mirror at the back of the bar: snowflakes. Calvin wiped the creeks of sweat from his face with his hanky. Snowflakes!

He tipped his glass and drank. He enjoyed drinking; he

liked the bitter sting of warm beer on his tongue, the small
bubbles needling his gullet, the taste of pickled nuts, a wash
of foam, and so on to yeasty fullness; four pints was a square
meal. He wasn't an alcoholic; he believed beer drinkers never
were. But he was almost certainly a drunkard. It was his choice,
not an affliction; it gave him pleasure.

"How far to Lilongwe?" He smacked his lips.

The dozing bartender stirred. "Lilongwe. Three-four days
on bicycle."

"How many miles?"

"Two hundred-so." The African shrugged. "You going that
side?"

"Today, I hope. I want to get the night bus to Blantyre."
Calvin sipped his beer. "This is my first trip north."

"You like?"

"Very nice," said Calvin. "You got a nice place here."

"Not like south," said the African. "No Osbong here."

"You mean no money?" Coins the value of a shilling were
called osbongs, after the head they wore.

"I am meaning," said the African, "no *Doctor* Osbong
bastard." He said it like the bird, "bustard".

Calvin went silent. He didn't talk politics, not there.

The African was staring at Calvin's glasses. "Good goggles,"
he said. "You buying here?"

"No, I got them from the States."

"America?"

"Yup."

"We hate Americans," said the African calmly. "They kill
black Negroes. Start trouble. Spy on us. Hate us too much.
Just big gangsters and cowboys up to now. That their badness.
Doctor Osbong say it good to trust Yankees. Myself I don't
trust at all. Osbong is" — the African squinted — "how you say
fisi in English?"

"Hyena," said Calvin. He put a ten-osbong note on the counter. "Have a beer."

"Eh!" the African kecked gratefully. "Happy Christmas, bwana. You with those soldiers?"

"Which soldiers?"

"In the trees," the African said.

"I'm an American," said Calvin. "I sell insurance — or, as you say in this neck of the woods, *assurance*."

"God," said the African, "made everyone the same. I take Guinness." He got himself a brown bottle and inserted a straw; and slurping, his lower lip rolled down showing bright pink, added, "For power, ha-ha."

"It's a good brew," said Calvin. He watched the African empty the bottle.

"Good goggles," said the African.

Jungle Lovers, 1971

No Christmas Ale In Antwerp

One of the Christmas delicacies which Belgian exiles, at all events those from Antwerp, will miss in England is English Christmas ale. So far as we know there is no special Christmas ale in England, but the famous Burton brewers export to Antwerp a special brew at Christmas-time. It is advertised as "Christmas ale", the English words, and the Belgians appreciate it highly. From their description it seems to be a rather stronger ale than the ordinary.

English beer has had a growing vogue in Antwerp, at all seasons of the year, for some time. There are three or four cafés or public-houses which sell only English beer. The first of them was an English public-house near the docks, intended, no doubt, for sailors or travellers from England. It sold English beer and British whisky, served English breakfasts of bacon and eggs, had an English landlady, and a very English name, the "George". Belgians discovered the "George", and began to go there for its excellent beer. It got quite a vogue, and another establishment specialising in English beer was opened near the railway station. This also scored a success, and we believe one or two others have been opened since. It is customary to serve with the beer a biscuit and a piece of English cheese (Belgian evidence does not specify what kind of cheese more particularly than that; it might be anything from Cheshire to double Gloucester).

The German occupation of Antwerp must have put a stop to the importation of English beer, but it increased the popularity of the English beer cafés. It was observed that the Germans never went to them, and that was quite enough to make them popular with Belgians, whatever the beer might be like. They felt free from surveillance there, and the cafés became fashionable accordingly. The "George", we believe, has been closed by the Germans since the occupation.

Brewer's Gazette, 17 December 1914

THE ROLLING ENGLISH ROAD

G.K. Chesterton

Before the Roman came to Rye or out to Severn strode,
The rolling English drunkard made the rolling English road.
A reeling road, a rolling road, that rambles round the shire,
And after him the parson ran, the sexton and the squire;
A merry road, a mazy road, and such as we did tread
The night we went to Birmingham by way of Beachy Head.
I knew no harm of Bonaparte and plenty of the Squire,
And for to fight the Frenchman I did not much desire;
But I did bash their baggonets because they came arrayed
To straighten out the crooked road an English drunkard made,
Where you and I went down the lane with ale-mugs in our
    hands,
The night we went to Glastonbury by way of Goodwin Sands.
His sins they were forgiven him; or why do flowers run
Behind him; and the hedges all strengthening in the sun?
The wild thing went from left to right and knew not which
    was which,
But the wild rose was above him when they found him in the
    ditch.
God pardon us, nor harden us; we did not see so clear
The night we went to Bannockburn by way of Brighton Pier.
My friends, we will not go again or ape an ancient rage,
Or stretch the folly of our youth to be the shame of age,
But walk with clearer eyes and ears this path that wandereth,
And see undrugged in evening light the decent inn of death;
For there is good news yet to hear and fine things to be seen,
Before we go to Paradise by way of Kensal Green.

1913

6

BEER AND FOOD

Without question, the greatest invention in the
history of mankind is beer. Oh, I grant you that the
wheel was also a fine invention, but the wheel does
not go nearly as well with pizza.

Dave Barry

BEER AND BREAD
MAKES THE CHEEKS RED

Elizabeth Craig

If there is one form of cookery that has been neglected more than another in Britain it is beer cookery. You have to go abroad to find housewives cooking freely with beer, and taking trouble about what they serve with it. There are plenty of books telling you about how to introduce wine to fare, but few extolling the flavour of beer; plenty of inns serving excellent beer, but not enough taking pains with its accompaniments; plenty of cocktail parties all the year round, but how few beer parties! And yet beer parties can be exciting.

Now what about arranging a beer party once in a while? It is an inexpensive form of entertainment, too long the monopoly of students. If your husband is, like mine, a beer-drinker, he will hail the idea.

In my time I have been a guest at many gay beer parties, but chiefly in Germany and the United States. One of the most amusing was held at a huge beer-garden in Berlin to celebrate the arrival of the dark malty brew called "Bock Beer". The guests sat at little tables drinking this beer, which is supposed to herald the spring, and munching pretzels and wafer-thin slices of black radishes dipped in salt to whet their appetite for more beer. In between rounds they danced with zest. We sat it out, men drinking beer and me "peach bowl", until a flamboyant couple who had been celebrating too liberally crashed into our table and we thought it a good excuse for slipping away.

On a New Year's morning, two years later, after bringing in the New Year in the Riessersee Hotel in Garmisch Partenkirchen, I sat entranced watching an English artist consuming with his German friends innumerable steaming white pork-and-veal sausages known as *Weisswurst*, and putting away quarts of beer, and I idly wondered as their voices rose and fell in praise of beer why one had to go to Germany to find hoteliers and restaurateurs making more of a fuss of the service of beer than they do in this country.

Remembering this, I was agreeably surprised when I received an invitation two summers ago to attend a beer party at Oxford, staged by the makers of a famous stout. There great care had been taken to serve cheese and kickshaws that team happily with beer. I would like to see all caterers who sell beer follow this example. It should be possible to get suitable snacks in every inn, at every public house, station buffet, and wherever else beer is on sale . . . That is why I have endeavoured in *Beer and Vittels* to pass on to you not only recipes for the use of beer in the kitchen, but also for some food that mates happily with beer.

"Beer and bread makes the cheeks red." It is a tonic for the weak and aged and an antidote for insomnia, so I am told. All through my wedded life I have been haunted by it in one or other of its many forms, which is my reward for marrying an ardent beer-drinker. When I'm below par, he says, "Why don't you take to stout?' When thirsty after a spell in the garden I cool with an iced drink: 'A Shandy would be better for you than that stuff.' When I have run out of beer and he wants a Welsh rarebit my name is mud, and I'm inclined to agree, for a Welsh rarebit without beer is to me an insipid affair.

If you should ask me what beer really means to me I would say a pleasant link with the traditions of the past. I cannot imagine a Britain without inns and the good companionship one has when lingering in old taverns over a pint of foaming beer. I also find that beer imparts a tang to numerous dishes, and consider that a cuisine that does not recognise the importance of beer in cooking is not a first-class cuisine. That is why I have taken the trouble to compile this little book on *Beer and Vittels*.

I dedicate it first of all to my husband, then to all other beer-lovers, and particularly to some Welch Fusiliers I remember with pleasure who used to sing to me in the First World War, and who always ended their sing-song with:

When I am dead, don't bury me at all
Just pickle my bones in alcohol
Put a bottle of beer at my head and feet
And then I know I'll rest complete.

I hope that in this Elizabethan age beer will become more potent and that its use in the kitchen will grow and grow. Britain without her beer would be a sorry place.

Beer and Vittels, 1955

THIS THANKSGIVING, GIVE THE BIRD A BEER

Lisa Morrison

Everywhere I look these days, there's another article about what wine to serve with Thanksgiving dinner.

If I see one more write-up about how Chardonnays go with cranberries, or how Merlot will make the meal, I think I am going to make like the turkeys and run for cover.

Que syrah, syrah! I am bucking the trend and going traditional this year.

I am serving beer.

After all, when the pilgrims sought a spot for their permanent landing in America, they did so, according to their diaries, because they ran out of beer on the *Mayflower*: "Our victuals being much spent, especially our beer," one diary read.

Apparently, in addition to finding shelter and food, some enterprising pilgrims set out to refurbish the beer supplies when the group first landed at Plymouth Rock. Perhaps these inventive immigrants used roots or tree bark for this inaugural ale, since the pilgrims obviously hadn't yet started growing grain. How much more traditional can you get than that?

So, it's with pilgrim pride that I will be guiding my guests through an exploration of beer and turkey with all the trimmings on this most American of holidays.

It's actually not as crazy as it sounds. With all the varieties of craft beer available in this land, beer really offers more tasty options than wine — from appetizers to that final slice of pumpkin pie.

"One of the most common things people ask a sommelier is, 'What wine goes with Thanksgiving dinner?' The answer is beer," says Garrett Oliver, brewmaster at Brooklyn Brewery in New York City, and author of *The Brewmaster's Table, Discovering the Pleasures of Real Beer with Real Food*.

The trick to matching beer with food, says Oliver, is to first "match up the impact on your palate." In other words, pair delicate foods with delicate beers, and heftier fare with beer that's got a little more "oomph" to it. Next, he says, match some of the flavours in the food with similar flavours in the beer. "I call this the 'flavour hook' — the part of the beer's flavour that links up directly with the flavour of the food," Garrett said at the Craft Brewers Conference in New Orleans. Caramel, coffee and, yes, even chocolate flavours prevail in many seasonal beers this time of year, making them easy to pair with traditional Thanksgiving fare.

Another trick: contrast the food with the beer. I find this works especially well with cloyingly rich foods laden with fat.

A slightly bitter beer (thanks to an extra dose of hops) will cut right through that fat, letting you enjoy some of the other flavours that might have gotten "lost" on your palate thanks to all that richness.

Of course, beer pairing, like wine pairing, is a bit subjective. But here are some course-by-course suggestions:

Salads and appetizers: Look for local, regional or imported wheat beers. Some words to search for include *weissbier*, *witbier*, *hefeweizen* and "American wheat beer." A German-style Kölsch or a crisp pilsner would also be a good choice. If you add blue cheese or nuts, try a locally or regionally brewed *doppelbock*. Another good "all-around" choice is an American pale ale or amber ale.

Turkey and trimmings: Roasting that turkey has created some interesting caramel (and, depending on the cook's prowess, some smoky) flavours, along with the nice herbal notes from the seasonings and stuffing. When enjoying beer with the bird, you have choices! Try a beer that matches those caramel notes, like an American amber ale, a *dubbel* or *tripel* (Belgian-style beers) or an Oktoberfest (there's a reason why they serve roasted chickens at the Oktoberfest in Munich). Or you can go for something that more closely supports the actual light meat and herbal seasonings of the turkey (and might even contrast with some of the fattier fare). Look for a locally brewed *bière de garde*, a Belgian-style *tripel* (many local and regional brewers make one) or a Belgian-style *saison*.

Mid-meal: I noticed that many wine stewards suggested a Champagne or sparkling wine to go with that "resting period" between the big meal and dessert. A beer that is created like Champagne is a recent emigrant to the United States. DeuS, Brut des Flanders, is brewed in Belgium and bottled in France using the *méthode Champagnoise*, thus marrying the best of the beer world with the best in wines. It is similarly priced to a good Champagne or sparkling wine, and worth every penny. If you want to wow your guests, try DeuS.

Dessert: Pumpkin pie, of course, is a natural. Try a local winter warmer or "spiced ale" as an accompaniment, or head over to the dark side of beer for a stout or porter. Oatmeal stouts, imperial stouts and roasty porters all provide enough chocolate and/or coffee goodness to support your dessert. Pecan pie? Same thing. Or add a Baltic porter, which is the rich cousin in the porter family.

Cheesecake? Try the above or add a Belgian-style fruity lambic like a *framboise* (raspberry flavored) or a *kriek* (cherry). Both are very good companions with chocolate, too.

Oh, and another thing — with the possible exception of the DeuS, you will be spending considerably less than wine for each 22-ounce to 750 ml bottle of beer you serve, making it even more enticing to try a few new ones along with your traditional foods.

One final note: I know many of these terms might not mean a lot to you right now, but remember when you didn't know how to say "Gewürztraminer"? Maybe you still don't. (I had to look up how to spell it to write this article.) It didn't stop you from picking up a bottle or two of wine for special meals. Don't let it stop you from exploring beer.

It might be a bit scary, yet exciting, embarking into this new realm. But like the pilgrims who first settled here on this fine land, you too can enter a brave new world this Thanksgiving by serving finely crafted domestic and imported beers at your table.

And what about those testy dinner guests who whine for wine? Tell 'em to put a cork in it.

Internet Broadcasting Systems, 2002

Filleted Steak And A Bottle Of Bass

Arnold Bennett

"Consommé Britannia," she began to read out from the menu, "Saumon d'Ecosse, Sauce Genoise, Aspics de Homard. Oh, heavens! Who wants these horrid messes on a night like this?"

"But, Nella, this is the best cooking in Europe," he protested.

"Say, father," she said, with seeming irrelevance, "had you forgotten it's my birthday to-morrow?"

"Have I ever forgotten your birthday, O most costly daughter?"

"On the whole you've been a most satisfactory dad," she answered sweetly, "and to reward you I'll be content this year with the cheapest birthday treat you ever gave me. Only I'll have it to-night."

"Well," he said, with the long-suffering patience, the readiness for any surprise, of a parent whom Nella had thoroughly trained, "what is it?"

"It's this. Let's have filleted steak and a bottle of Bass for dinner to-night. It will be simply exquisite. I shall love it."

"But my dear Nella," he exclaimed, "steak and beer at Felix's! It's impossible! Moreover, young women still under twenty-three cannot be permitted to drink Bass."

"I said steak and Bass, and as for being twenty-three, shall be going in twenty-four to-morrow."

Miss Racksole set her small white teeth.

There was a gentle cough. Jules stood over them. It must have been out of a pure spirit of adventure that he had selected this table for his own services. Usually Jules did not personally wait at dinner. He merely hovered observant, like a captain on the bridge during the mate's watch. Regular frequenters of the hôtel felt themselves honoured when Jules attached himself to their tables.

Theodore Racksole hesitated one second, and then issued the order with a fine air of carelessness: "Filleted steak for two, and a bottle of Bass." It was the bravest act of Theodore Racksole's life, and yet at more than one previous crisis a high courage had not been lacking to him.

"It's not in the menu, sir," said Jules the imperturbable.

"Never mind. Get it. We want it."

"Very good, sir."

Jules walked to the service-door, and, merely affecting to look behind, came immediately back again.

"Mr Rocco's compliments, sir, and he regrets to be unable to serve steak and Bass to-night, sir."

"Mr Rocco?" questioned Racksole lightly.

"Mr Rocco," repeated Jules with firmness.

"And who is Mr Rocco?"

"Mr Rocco is our chef, sir." Jules had the expression of a man who is asked to explain who Shakespeare was.

The two men looked at each other. It seemed incredible that Theodore Racksole, the ineffable Racksole, who owned a thousand miles of railway, several towns, and sixty votes in Congress, should be defied by a waiter, or even by a whole hôtel. Yet so it was. When Europe's effete back is against the wall not a regiment of millionaires can turn its flank.

Jules had the calm expression of a strong man sure of victory. His face said: "You beat me once, but not this time, my New York friend!"

As for Nella, knowing her father, she foresaw interesting events, and waited confidently for the steak. She did not feel hungry, and she could afford to wait.

The Grand Babylon Hotel, 1902

ALE-WYFES AND BEER CHEFS

Lucy Saunders

Archaeological records from about 8000BC prove the existence of fermentation. In fact, the most ancient recipe yet
discovered is a collection of Sumerian stone tablets engraved
with methods to bake bread and use the loaves to ferment a
drink "which makes anyone who tastes it feel blissful and
exhilarated." Ahhh, beer.

By the time the Domesday Book was compiled in England
in 1086 AD, brewing was an established part of domestic life
across settlements in the northern hemisphere, as well as parts
of South America and middle Asia. As a safe alternative to
water from polluted rivers, wells or cisterns, beer added flavour
and nutrition. It was a dietary staple, so cooking with beer was
convenient — as often the household's cook did the brewing,
too. In England, this is how the moniker alewyfe, came to be.
The Tudor era in England was when a quart of ale was renowned
as "a dish fit for a king" in Shakespeare's *A Winter's Tale*.

What recipes are available for cooking with beer?
Documented recipes naturally follow education, literacy, and
the growth of printing. By the 16th century, cookbooks for
the English gentry had reached the wealthy middle classes,
inspiring culinary creativity.

Take Ale and set it on the fire, and when it seetheth scum
it, and then put in your Sparrowes and small Raisins,
Sugar and Sinamon, Ginger and Date, and let them boyle
together, and then take marrows or Butter, and a little
Vergiuos, and keepe it close. And when it is enough, make
sops in platters and serve them forth.

A Book of Cookrye, AW, 1591

About five per cent of the recipes catalogued for *Cooking with Shakespeare* use ale in some form, according to co-author Mark Morton. "It was common to cook with beer as it was easy to get," says Morton. "In Queen Elizabeth's court, everyone was allotted a gallon and a half of small beer per day."

The low-gravity ales of about 2.5% alcohol by volume were often brewed with spices most complementary to cooking: sweet gale, coriander, fennel, or the more costly ginger, cloves, and grains of paradise, imported from Asia.

> Take a legge of mutton and cutte it in small slices and put it in a chafter and put thereto a pottell of ale, and scome it clene, then put thereto seven or eighte onions thin sliced and after thei have boylde one houre put therto a disshe of swete butter and so let theim boyle till thei be tender and then put therto a litle peper and salte.

A Propre New Booke of Cokery, Anon., 1545

Food and beer found their places at tables high and low. Ale and beer were essential foodstuffs, consumed as liquid nourishments by persons of all ages and classes and used in both cooking and healing. In a 16th-century ledger from the estate of the Duke of Clarence in Northumberland, records show that the high consumption of beer for the household of almost 300 people (more than half of them servants) made it an economic necessity to brew on site. Some exceptions existed, mostly for royal households close by monastery breweries.

The monastic brewing tradition set beer's place at those tables, even if served as "liquid bread". Ale was often used to cook eggs, as in possets and the 14th-century recipe for "caudles". Sops, possets and soups made with beer and cream also appear. Melted cheese mixed with ale and served over toasted bread was a staple dish called a Welsh rarebit, or Welsh rabbit.

Another iconic combination, the beer cheese soup, might have descended from the beer and heavy cream soups favoured in Scandinavia and Denmark. (This might account for the popularity of beer and cheese soup in northern regions of the USA which were largely settled by immigrants from these countries. Wisconsin beer cheese soup is a perfect pairing of two of the state's top agricultural products.)

Belgian monasteries are famous for innovations in beer and brewing, and sometimes used beer as an ingredient, mostly rind-washed cheeses made with ale. Belgian monasteries began brewing in the early 10th century, but the restricted diets of monastic life served food as simply prepared as possible, in order not to incite any overly carnal desires!

from "Ale-Wyfes & Beer-Chefs: The Evolution of Cooking with Beer", 2009

THE NEAREST THING TO EATING BEER

Sue Nowak

While Belgian food is made *with* beer, Austrian and Bavarian foods are made *for* beer. From the Tyrol to Munich, it's a great, galumphing cuisine of million-calorie platters matched by giant steins.

Bier hall décor echoes the cuisine — big and brazen: hefty wooden tables flanked by rough benches in huge halls with weighty beams and roaring fires; just the ambience for comfort food and drink to cock a snook at winter.

It's a region of fat liver dumplings, fist-thick salty pretzels, steaming sauerkraut and long-proved dark loaves (the nearest thing you'll come to eating beer). Best of all are the parts of the pig that go so well with both pale wheats and chewy dark *dunkels* — smoked sausages, cured hams, whole black puddings simmered in stock and belly pork roasted until the fat snaps away to leave snapping crisp crackling.

En route to our holiday in the area we stopped off in Strasbourg, where the medieval old town was reminiscent of Bruges, and the food, just as hearty, put our digestive systems on alert.

By luck, we stumbled into Le Baeckeoffe d'Alsace, a "*winstub*" named after its house special, the stew to end all stews. Topped by a layer of thinly sliced crisp potatoes it looked for all the world like a Lancashire hotpot. Beneath were chunks of pork, beef and lamb simmered for hours with onions in a stock I thought was wheat beer but turned out to be the local white wine served, like the beer, in jugs.

Our other dish, though, did have hop character: described as braised pig's knuckle, it turned out to be pork hock basted to a varnish veneer in a dark beer. Absolutely delicious — but disconcerting to have caught the eye of the accordion player, who kept sidling up and serenading us, to the amusement of the other diners . . .

In the mountains 50 miles south of Salzburg we stayed in a pre-season deserted ski resort, Radstadt, where the great, empty hotel — bar, restaurant and swimming pool eerily deserted and patrolled by an Alsatian the size of a wolf — was scarily reminiscent of *The Shining*. Returning through the churchyard at midnight after a *dunkel* too many we found a newly-dug grave, earth piled alongside, waiting to receive its occupant on the morrow . . .

But the welcome in the family-run village inn, reached by footbridge, was warm and boisterous — as was the menu.

Genuine local dishes were enjoyed by villagers who gathered to play cards and wrap themselves round steaming platefuls washed down by a surprisingly wide range of beers, both bottled and draught.

Here were big bowls of fortifying soul made with the most intense stock I've tasted outside a Chinese restaurant. But where the Chinese go for subtlety, these were robust, thick with noodles, chunks of vegetables, sliced frankfurters and solid little potato dumplings.

Slices of both smoked and unsmoked pork arrived with bread dumplings the size of tennis balls, one plain, one stuffed with minced veal. A thick slice of belly pork was served on hot sauerkraut garnished with a frivolous rampant frankfurter in the shape of a sausage dog; half a litre of amber Paulaner Hefeweizen made the perfect accompaniment.

From our mountain eyrie we took the train to Salzburg for a serious trencherman's day.

Lunchtime was spent dining both wisely and too well at the Zipfer Bierhaus in the market place, where we demolished serious platefuls of bierwurst (once made from ham marinated in beer — alas, not now) and a classic thin pork schnitzel fried in breadcrumbs, while downing litres of pale, surprisingly hoppy draught Zipfer Urtyp, followed by the malty Christmas Dunkel Weizen. Well, we were saving ourselves for the evening . . .

That was when we took the steep, chilly walk to the Augustiner Brauhaus hall. Through an archway, along a dimly lit, cobbled alley, we found giant doors opening into a marble-slabbed echoing vestibule. Did a pub really lurk somewhere in these sepulchral surroundings, more in keeping with the brewery's monastic origins?

But as we walked along a high vaulted hall, from far away came the sound of merry-making. We followed it down a wide stone staircase into a gigantic crypt-like cellar packed with scores of serious drinkers, and waiters delivering fistfuls of steins of superb, malty bock.

The food arrangements were novel. In the adjoining corridor little deli-style serveries were set into the wall — you filled your plate with seed-encrusted rye batons and cheese at one (we went for a fudge-like local type the colour of caramel, perfect with the beer), olives and gherkins at another, hot smoked bockwurst and pork rissoles at a third, smoked fish and pickled herrings and so on.

On the first leg of our journey back we visited Kufstein at the insistence of a CAMRA friend, who said we would find "the second best bar in Europe". We did. It was closed. Happily the adjoining 500-year-old Batzenhaust was not only blessed with superb Bavarian cooking, but a respectable selection of beers as well. It also had something I never expect to see again — a coin-operated copper and brass rinks dispense on a long wood arm that you could swing around the room, choosing anything from beer to schnapps. We played safe and had draught winter Doppelbock to accompany black pudding, liver sausage, smoke pork and potatoes, and a white cabbage side salad flavoured with dill seeds.

In Munich that night we allowed ourselves to marvel at the spectacle of the Hofbrauhaus beer hall where, it seemed, thousands were quaffing steins of the malty house bock, before crossing to Ayinger brewery's restaurant — and one of the finest restaurants of our trip.

With six house beers on the list, we began with a sparkling, spritzy wheat beer made with 50% wheat malt to accompany Bavarian feast day soup packed with semolina dumplings and liver noodles, and a creamed horseradish soup surely invented for wheat beer.

With my main course, belly and loin pork in dark wheat beer sauce accompanied by light-as-air white bread dumpling and a potato dumpling like a cannon ball, I drank a big-bodied, spicy winter *dunkel* the colour of the burnished pretzels in the bread basket.

As a footnote we spent our last night in Luxembourg where an organic market was in full swing. In pride of place was a trailer from the tiny Okult brewery at nearby Redange, plying shoppers with Belgian-style wheat beer, a Bavarian bock and, would you believe, an English inspired stout!

Beer magazine, February 2004

INDIAN-SPICED CRAB CAKES

Garrett Oliver, Brooklyn Brewery

Sweet crab meat and the heat of the curry and jalapeño are perfectly complemented by the malts and hop character of Brooklyn East India Pale Ale.

INGREDIENTS
1 medium red onion, peeled and sliced
1 jalapeño pepper, stemmed
1 red bell pepper, cored
½ lb lump crab meat, cooked
1 lightly beaten egg
1 tablespoon mayonnaise
1 teaspoon grated fresh ginger
1 heaping tablespoon curry powder
1 teaspoon cumin
juice of one big lemon
small handful of cilantro, with stems
1 ½ cups of Japanese panko bread crumbs

1. Mince together, as finely as you have patience for, the onion, jalapeño, the bell pepper, and the cilantro. When you're done, it shouldn't look chunky anymore.

2. In a bowl, combine the mixture with the crab meat, egg, mayo, ginger, curry powder, cumin, and lemon juice. Add in ½ cup of panko bread crumbs, mix thoroughly.

3. Taste the mixture, then salt to taste. If you want them spicier, you can add some of your favorite hot sauce and blend it in.

4. With your hands, form your crab cakes into small patties, then press more bread crumbs onto the surfaces of the patties. Put them on a plate, cover them and put them into the refrigerator.

5. When it's time to cook them, all you're doing is frying them until they turn golden brown on one side, then flipping them over and browning the other side. This will take you maybe 10 minutes.

6. Serve with a snappy India pale ale like our East India Pale Ale; they work wonders with Indian and Thai spices.

Now I Know Why They Call It The "High" Table

Michael Jackson

Profiles of the great and the good frequently allude to the rituals of Oxbridge as though we are all familiar with them having spent our formative years by the Isis or the Cam. Those of us who didn't are left to puzzle over the magic that produces authors, High Court judges and Cabinet ministers. With our noses to the mullioned window, we seek the significance of the manner in which the dreamingly cellared claret is decanted, the direction in which the crusted port is passed at High Table.

The other day I was invited to dinner at an Oxford college. It was a chance to study the social behaviour of those with their fingertips on the glittering prizes.

I was greeted with a dog's nose — there has been much debate as to the proper composition of a dog's nose, ever since Dickens raised the question in *The Pickwick Papers*. "A glass of ale with a dash of gin, a popular sailors' drink in the British Navy," suggests *Cocktails and How to Mix Them* (price 21/6d), an undated work whose author is identified only as "Robert", late of the Embassy Club, London, and the Casino Municipal, "two parts porter to one part gin - not recommended", warns the 1948 work *The Fine Art of Mixing Drinks* by David Embraury, an American. "A measure of gin, topped up with a filtered Bavarian wheat beer," pronounced Martin Wilka, outgoing president of the Oxford University Beer Appreciation Society, handing me a champagne flute containing the drink.

The blend of juniper and wheat was appetizingly dry, like a tart alcoholic ginger ale. Before sitting down to the keenly awaited dinner, I was asked if I would like another drink. Perhaps a Belgian beer, a Rodenbach Alexander, matured in oak and flavoured with cherry essence? I settled for the Watou "White Beer", spiced with orange peel and coriander, and named after the village near Ypres where it is made. This beer was served with, and used in the preparation of, the first course, a juicy-tasting leek mousse.

This was the annual dinner of the society. The main course was described as Oxford John Steak, which turned out to be cut from leg of lamb. It was presented in a caper sauce, and served with a glass of the fruity-tasting Varsity Ale, made by Oxford's local brewery, Morrell's.

Then came excellent Cheddar and Stilton cheeses, superbly accompanied by the smokey, almost whisky-ish, Black Wych Stout from a tiny brewery in nearby Witney.

Dessert was sticky toffee pudding both prepared and served with the very strong (8.5 per cent) Douglas Scotch Ale, brewed in Edinburgh but sold only in France. This was almost as toffeeish as the pudding.

Our digniuf was another strong brew, the warming College Ale, again from Morrell's. This was presented with a bowl of walnuts.

The after-dinner repartee touched lightly upon matters of such consequence as barn-dancing and high-powered motorcycles, but the real excitement concerned a proposed visit by the society to some breweries in Belgium.

There were two dons at my table. "I still quite like Old Peculier," one observed to me. "Unfortunately, I am a South African," said the other, "so I prefer lager."

"I have visited three breweries in two terms," announced a contented Andrew Clyde, a philosophy student. He meant to add a shaft of Cartesian wit, but I restrained him, despite the menace of his kilt pin, which was decorating a waistcoat in the McCallum tartan.

Lucy Masterton, who is studying biochemistry, was worried that an admirer might spill his Orval Trappist Ale on her nifty black two-piece. Ms Masterton wanted to tell me about her holiday in the United States. She built her itinerary around a visit to the Catamount Brewery, in White River Junction, Vermont. As her mind filled with the recollection of Catamount's golden ale, she shuddered to think that she had once enjoyed "cider and sweet drinks".

Jack Hemens, a student of philosophy, politics and economics, sported a pony-tail and a cigar and told me that he had bought his first beer at the age of 14. "I cycled to a cricket match in the country, had a pint of bitter, and thought, 'This is the way to be'. There is something about bitter . . . by the sixth-form, I was comparing flavours in different brews." Dan Smithers, with hair of more than shoulder length and a red cummerbund, a graduate in engineering and computing science, was introduced to me as a star home-brewer who produces the best wheat beer in Oxford. A comparative tasting of wheat beers is a future event on the society's agenda. Another is an attempt to restore the tradition of every college having its own ale.

Oxford's origins lie in a convent, and later in monasteries, followed by colleges; all, in the manner of the times, brewed beer for their own dining tables. Monks are believed to have made beer in at least the 1400s on Swan Nest Island, the site of a commercial brewery from 1590, and of the Morrell family's business since 1743. The last college breweries fizzled out after the Second World War.

The memory lingers on in the name Brasenose College. According to the 1870 *Dictionary of Phrase and Fable*, by the aptly-named Reverend S. C. Brewer, this derives from the Old Flemish *brasenhuis*, meaning brewhouse. The nose-shaped door-knocker at the college is a visual pun.

In a similar flourish, gilded lions holding sprigs of clover, part of the family's heraldry, guard the wrought-iron arch that is the gateway to Morrell's brewery. The oldest parts of the brewery's structure date from 1645, although there is an Elizabethan look to the 1880s buildings that predominate.

A stream now tumbles idly over Morrell's weir and past its water-wheel, and a pair of ducks go for meals of spilled barley-malt in the yard. "Beware of the ducks," a large sign warns draymen.

Inside, two tabbies, Mum and Fatcat, hunt any mice that may further deplete the grain supply. Malt from nearby Wallingford and hops from Worcester meet hard water from the Cotswolds and Chilterns in two copper brew-kettles, one dating from 1898, the other having begun life as a whisky still in Scotland in 1935.

Two tiny copper fermenting vessels, a tenth of the usual size, are kept aside for the small brews of College Ale. My own favourite beer from Morrell's is an intensely malty one called Graduate. Like a truly old-fashioned local brewery, Morrell's sells the lion's share of its beer in its own pubs: there are 140 of them, all within 20 to 30 miles of Oxford.

It is the smaller, newer, local rival, the brewery in Witney, that has to be entrepreneurial and expansionist. This brewery is called Wychwood, after a nearby medieval forest. It was founded in 1983, and is soon to move to new premises on the site of a long-extinct old brewery.

Wychwood has 17 pubs, with such names as Hobgoblin, Doctor Thirsty's and Howling Wolf, stretched across southern England between Brighton and Bristol. Its most distinctive beer, full of happy freshness, is unappetisingly described as the Dog's Bollocks. This is apparently a colloquial term of approval.

Having never been partial in the Boat Race, but now discovering an affinity with the dark blue, I shall try to find a pint as I cheer for Oxford. Whether or not I shall have the balls to ask for it by name is another question. It doesn't seem the kind of expression one uses at High Table.

Independent, March 1994

7

THE MEANING OF BEER

Sometimes when I reflect on all the beer I drink,
I feel ashamed. Then I look into the glass and think about
the workers in the brewery and all of their hopes and
dreams. If I didn't drink this beer, they might be out
of work and their dreams would be shattered. I think,
"It is better to drink this beer and let their dreams come
true than be selfish and worry about my liver."

Babe Ruth

INSPECTOR MORSE IN THE PEEP OF DAWN

Colin Dexter

The Peep of Dawn (as engagingly named a pub as Morse could remember) boasted only one bar, with wooden wall-seats, and after finding out from the landlord which bitter the locals drank he sat with his pint in the window alcove and supped contentedly. He wasn't quite sure whether his own oft-repeated insistence that he could always think more lucidly after an extra ration of alcohol was wholly true. He certainly *believed* it to be true, though; and quite certainly many a breakthrough in previous investigations had been made under such attendant circumstances. It was only in recent months that he had found himself querying his earlier assumption about such a *post hoc, ergo propter hoc* proposition; and it had occasionally occurred to him that fallacious logic was not infrequently the offspring of wishful thinking. Yet for Morse (and he quite simply accepted the fact) the world *did* invariably seem a much warmer, more manageable place after a few pints of beer; and quite certainly he knew that (for himself, at any rate) it was on such occasions that the imaginative processes usually *started*. It may have been something to do with the very *liquidity* of alcohol, for he had often seen these processes in terms of just such a metaphor. It was as if he were lulled and sitting idly on the sea-front, and watching, almost entranced, as some great Master of the Tides drew in the foam-fringed curtains of the waters towards his feet and then pulled them back in slow retreat to the creative era.

The Secret of Annexe 3, 1986

STRONG BEER

Robert Graves

"What do you think
The bravest drink
Under the sky?"
"Strong beer," said I.
"There's a place for everything,
Everything, anything,
There's a place for everything
Where it ought to be:
For a chicken, the hen's wing;
For poison, the bee's sting;
For almond-blossom, Spring;
A beerhouse for me."
"There's a prize for every one
Every one, any one,
There's a prize for every one,
Whoever he may be:
Crags for the mountaineer,
Flags for the Fusilier,
For English poets, beer!
Strong beer for me!"

"Tell us, now, how and when
We may find the bravest men?"
"A sure test, an easy test:
Those that drink beer are the best,
Brown beer strongly brewed,
English drink and English food."
Oh, never choose as Gideon chose
By the cold well, but rather those

Who look on beer when it is brown,
Smack their lips and gulp it down.
Leave the lads who tamely drink
With Gideon by the water brink,
But search the benches of the Plough,
The Tun, the Sun, the Spotted Cow,
For jolly rascal lads who pray,
Pewter in hand, at close of day,
"Teach me to live that I may fear
The grave as little as my beer."

Fairies and Fusiliers, 1918

PINT-SIZED

Jonathan Meades

I spent the 1950s in pub car parks. In summer I kicked gravel, walked parlously on wall tops, scaled trees. In winter which is what it usually was I sat in my father's car watching my breath condense, miming driving (Collins, Hawthorn), scrutinising the underside of Issigonis's dashboards, reading maps. Irrespective of season I ate crisps, drank fizzy lemonade, dreamt but not so much that I forget the day in '56 when my father discovered that Messrs Smith of Cricklewood had increased the price of a packet of crisps from 3d to 4d; still, there was no diminution of his generosity.

Irrespective of season, what I did mostly was wait. I waited longest outside pubs near Evesham, pubs beside the Avon, pubs beneath Bredon Hill, pubs with fruitholdings and hop gardens all around them, pubs with their own foot ferries, pubs of immemorial beams and bricks.

I waited longest there because my mother, antipathetic to my father's family, rarely accompanied us to his home town, to the Edwardian past that was my grandmother's perpetual present, to drink with his strange brothers my uncles, to eat grey beef at three. The stink of the gusts of the bars whose doors I steeled myself to put my head round, trying to catch a familial eye, was invariable. Grown-up life smelt bad, stale, fungal, fusty. Grown-ups breathed pea-soupers, motes floated in their exhalations, the many-denier opacity of the air combined with its stench to make me humble back to the car, unnoticed and crispless.

My retreat was, I knew, from beer, from beer's quarry, from beer's sites, from the intense jocularity it fostered. Sure, there are gin palaces and cider bothies but that English peculiarity and institution, the public house, is founded in beer. Beverage and building are mutually dependent. To dislike one was to dislike the other. To dislike either was, in my uncles' eyes at any rate, to abjure a rite of entry into adulthood.

The Boy's First Pint was about as close as middle-class, middle-century, middle England got to the bar mitzvah. Anglicanism may have been strong on piety, on body-and-blood baloney, on tiresome porkies about Mary's immaculacy and the resurrection, but it was typically shy about hormonal mayhem, about initiation into adulthood. Anglican First Communion comprised taking the worst that bakery and viticulture could offer from a paedophile's papery hands in the grim fastness of a cathedral; it was a ceremony that signified nothing. The First Pint, on the other hand, was a main line to an older, deeper England, to John Barleycorn, to the very land in which had grown the cereal, to the stout yeomanry that had cultivated it.

That, anyway, was the gist of the avuncular spiel. These two solitaries were not in thrall to the Anglican god but to a

home-made pantheism in which *veldtschoen*, Richard Jeffries'
Bevis, Housman, tweed, arts and crafts, Vaughan Williams,
cleft sticks, *Stalky and Co.*, *The Countryman*, Social Credit, Aertex,
Chesterton, xenophobia, the Malverns and baked hedgehog
all played a part. Beer was sacramental.

I wondered: it wasn't merely that I couldn't stand the taste
of the stuff. I was not keen to buy into this maypole mysticism:
I didn't ever want to join. Besides, beer was more than sacra-
ment to my father's elder brother; it was, albeit indirectly, his
livelihood. He was town clerk of Burton upon Trent, brewery
to the nation, brewery to the Baltic, brewery to the Empire
and ne plus ultra of the single industry town.

Burton was beer. It was ale stores, cooperages, malt houses,
a high incidence of sclerosis of the liver, Bass's private narrow-
gauge railway, Bass's almshouses, Bass's many churches. It was
all brick, stylistically sober, monumental. And H. Turner
Meades presided over its self-destruction. I guess he knew
no better. His vision of England was profoundly anti-urban
(which begs the question: what was he doing in such a job?)
and he was generationally conventional in his distaste for
Victorian architecture.

He and the councillors he despised and the brewers he
sucked up to would have seen no virtues in hundred-year-
old industrial buildings. Especially not in the white heat of
the Keg Era: that sort of beer, no nicer and no nastier than
the preceding stuff, I thought then was the brewing industry's
contribution to '60s neophilia. This was the beer of the future.
Soon the world would be all monorails and robots, and non-
iron suits with no lapels, and colonies in space. And we'd toast
our progress in Red Barrel and Party Sixes and Pipkins.

When I say we, I evidently exclude myself because the First
Pint was still undrunk, and likely to remain so. And so long as
it did, I knew very well that, *pace* developments to my balls and

my voice, I should remain stranded at the portals of English manhood. I rather suspect that I'm still there; it wasn't until I found myself in Belfort at the age of fifteen that I tasted beer I actually wanted to drink.

Belfort is not in England. It is in France's non-cricket-playing republic. Beer there was free of quasi-eucharistic mystique; it was not a bibulous salute to the religiose nationalism of Barrès to a foreign teenager, it was just a pleasant bevvy, one which was not habitually drunk in quantity, and certainly not for oblivion. That state could be otherwise achieved. Beer and its derivatives are vastly impractical agents of intoxication, and dangerous ones, too, more dangerous than distilled liquors which are, infamously, more heavily taxed, more dangerous than hashish and unadulterated opiates.

The English have been made to suffer more in the inevitable and universal quest for intoxication than have the peoples of less proscriptively governed countries. What might appear to be volumetric masochism is state-prompted sadism. Addiction to beer is indicated by various vitamin B deficiencies, pseudo-dropsical traits such as hanging jowls and guest symptom wet beriberi. The point is this: spirits and, to an evidently lesser extent, wine effect intoxication in quantities which do not fool the body into believing that it is being fed. The copious amounts of beer required to achieve this end do just that.

My specialist adviser on this topic, Professor Guy Neild of Middlesex Hospital, warns that beer is so wanting in proteins that "drinking enough to get pissed is like eating sugar all day". He adds that vast quantities of alcohol are harmless provided the patient pursues a decent diet. Beer discourages that pursuit. Or, rather, the way that the English and the rest of Europe and the rest of northern Europe drink it discourages simultaneous guzzling not least because food, other than thirst promoters such as crisps, inhibits bibulous appetite.

It might be argued that beer is the enemy of food and that a country in which beer has primacy is bound to suffer culinary impoverishment; Belgium is the lone exception. And the gastronomic burgeoning in this country over the past couple of decades has coincided with, has perhaps been pushed by, the ever-increasing availability of affordable wines. But beer is culturally potent, its example is unforgotten; the English now drink wine as though it was beer, without food, standing up, at parties. Same mistake, different bev. Imported bev, too — a fact that might be used to emphasise the fragile base on which this fresh gastronomy is founded.

Sure, there is English wine and, yes, the Romans, unhampered by the knowledge vouchsafed to celebrity weather girls, did cultivate the grape as far north as Lincoln. This is not, though, a vinous country; it produces only white wine. And a vineyard in Surrey — you are thinking, rightly, of the one just north of Dorking on the A24 — is as marvellously freakish, as admirably inapposite as, say, the mosque at Woking which the beer victim Ian Nairn (fourteen pints per lunchtime, latterly) described as "extraordinarily dignified". Both mosque and vineyard are untempered by location. The mosque is by an unknown Sunderland architect, W. I. Chambers; the vineyard is by its proprietors. The vineyard is an intruder, a hop garden isn't.

The Englishness I eschewed, the Englishness of my uncles, may be an unembraced faith but the integrity of the landscape which underpins that faith is sort of sacred. The ordered, ranked, fructous lines of Worcestershire and the Weald touch me in a way that my native Downs don't. Those downs are good for mutton and as canvases on which to represent the optimistic ideal of manhood (the Cerne Giant), hippofetishism (everywhere), Anzac bereavement (Fovant). They don't connect. Oast houses and hop kilns do. It doesn't matter that they are all now houses, domestic dwellings.

As I grow older, I am more and more inclined to some sort of concordance with the blight I was born to: against my will I'm sucked into a terminally English appreciation of the terminally English medium of watercolour which is as weak as beer, an analogue of it, and the means by which our scapes and architecture are best represented. Depictions of Wealden oast houses by Rowland Hilder strike some pre-aesthetic part of the brain; I find myself dorsally thrilled by places whose like Henry James called "deepest England", places whose abundance and arboreal richness informs Michael Powell's *A Canterbury Tale*, the country around Goudhurst, the majestic intimacy of Fawsley, where Warwickshire, Northamptonshire and Oxfordshire collide; the Marches seen from Clee Hill. To drink anything other than beer in these places would be a solecism, an act of ingestive treachery, dead wrong.

Beer is unescapable, the way nationhood is, the way the poor are. Beer assails us — there is no building type so common as the public house, apart, that is, from the private dwelling. There are getting on for 100,000 of them in this country, a figure which stands as some sort of indictment of the collective taste. And for every exuberant gross-out like the Philharmonic between Liverpool's cathedrals there are hundreds of dismal city pubs. And for every forgotten treasure like the room with two barrels and an out-of-date KP ad beside the Severn at Ashleworth, the Boat Inn, there are hundreds of dumps in the sticks hosted by bonhomous pint-raisers. Here, let's raise a glass to olde Englande, a glass of crème de menthe with a Sambuca top.

For it's olde Englande to which pubs belong, to which they increasingly belong. The apogee of pub architecture was, roughly, 1880 to 1910; I'm not referring to inn architecture or hotel architecture, but specifically to boozers, purpose-built to intoxicate and, incidentally, to delight.

Imagine the gulf between a mean terraced house and these palaces, erected by brewers for their people, their subjects. Bevelled glass, mahogany, abundant carving, marble, velvet — these are the materials of brassy sybaritism. The great pubs were wonderlands, fantastical playgrounds, stages of easy exoticism: their decorative richness assisted intoxication, they transported their customers. They offered more than merely liquid escapism.

And that persisted during the only subsequent era of pub architecture that is of much moment. The roadhouse belongs to motoring's first age, when cars were a pleasure rather than a chore, when the now quaint idea of driving to a beer hangar beside an arterial road was reckoned a good one. These predominantly outer-suburban boozers were rigged out in period styles from the great dressing-up box of architecture's past.

Now and again you'll come upon an essay in the international modern style — the Comet at Hatfield or the Prospect Inn at Minster-in-Thanet — but usually it was full-blown Tudor or Wars of the Roses or Dutch Renaissance or Quality Street Regency. The place to see this stuff in its blowzy ripeness is Birmingham where two great breweries, Mitchell & Butler and Ansells, competed to produce ever larger, ever more theatrical pubs which were, if you like, hoardings for themselves — they had to be big enough to catch the eye of the passing motorist.

The stylistic revivalism of these places is light-hearted; you can imagine Errol Flynn swinging across them. There is no intention to deceive. Pastiche not fakery was the rule. That is no longer the case. As the production of beer is increasingly executed in plants which have no technical or architectural kinship with the sort of building we readily identify as a brewery, so do the places where beer is sold and consumed advance with increasing alacrity into the past. A past which is realised with dour solemnity.

All the theme pubs of the '70s and '80s – the Colditz pubs and the car rally pubs and the crazy cottage pubs – have disappeared. Brewers large and small have only one theme today, and that is a simulacrum of yesterday. It's as though they know that bibulous solace is only to be found in some illusory "heritage". It's not much of a prospect – wrong word, that.

1994

A GOOD GLASS OF PORTER

Thomas Mann

So he grew up; in wretched weather, in the teeth of wind and mist, grew up, so to say, in a yellow mackintosh, and, generally speaking, he throve. A little anaemic he had always been, so Dr Heidekind said, and had him take a good glass of porter after third breakfast every day, when he came home from school. This, as everyone knows, is a hearty drink – Dr Heidekind considered it a blood-maker – and certainly Hans Castorp found it most soothing to his spirits and encouraging to a propensity of his, which his Uncle Tienappel called "dozing": namely, sitting staring into space, with his jaw dropped and his thoughts fixed on just nothing at all. But on the whole he was sound and fit, an adequate tennis player and rower; though actually handling the oars was less to his taste than sitting of a summer evening on the terrace of the Uhlenhorst ferry-house, with a good drink before him and the sound of music in his ears, while he watched the lighted boats, and the swans mirrored in the bright water.

The Magic Mountain, 1924

CRAFT BEER

Evan Rail

I was having a great time at a craft beer festival in Berlin, Germany, when I suddenly realized that I didn't know what craft beer meant any more.

This was both highly inconvenient and somewhat surprising, because until that point I was pretty confident I knew at least something about beer, and because a number of people were relying upon my confidence in that knowledge, if not the knowledge itself. I had been invited to Berlin to judge the city's very first craft beer festival, something which I had mistakenly thought to be no problem at all: I had travelled fairly extensively in Germany, researching beer just about everywhere I could find it. I had a long feature on *zoigl*, a rare beer style from the hinterlands of Germany's Oberpfalz region, in the can but not yet published at *Saveur* magazine. I had travelled to Aufsess, the Bavarian town that claims to have the world's highest number of breweries per capita, and I had walked the local brewery trail there with my wife and our young son. I had just written a long article in the *New York Times* about the arrival of good beer in Berlin, as well as another on the return of the city's indigenous beer style, *Berliner weisse*, for *All About Beer*. Before my train pulled into the Hauptbahnhof, I was pretty sure I was up to the job.

That job entailed evaluating every beer at the festival, buying samples from each brewery's stand and trying to select the best while I wandered around in the sun, chatting with friends. (As far as jobs go, this one is pretty pleasurable. I highly recommend you check it out yourself if you get the chance.) The event was taking place in an abandoned train yard in the former East Berlin neighbourhood of Friedrichshain, and I wove around the graffiti-covered, century-old brick buildings, tasting beers, making observations and writing up notes.

Unlike most thoughts which involve immoderate amounts of alcohol, after a few hours I started to have a very clear understanding that there was something unusual about all the beers I was tasting. Instead of what I would have thought of as Germany's native craft brews, virtually every option I tasted that day was an imitation of an American craft beer, a local take on something from Sierra Nevada, Deschutes or Stone.

I went through my notes again and looked over the list of what I'd tasted. Beers like the rich Kathi-Bräu dark lager from Aufsess? Not at the festival. Any version of *zoigl*? Not at the festival. Smokey Schlenkerla from Bamberg? Not at the festival. The only traditional German craft brewery at the festival appeared to be Schneider Weisse, which probably got a pass because it had once brewed a hoppy *weizen* in collaboration with Brooklyn Brewery, the renowned American craft producer. Everything else seemed to be American-inspired: either a hoppy pale ale, an IPA, a double IPA, a Russian imperial stout, or some other American craft style.

I grabbed a delicious coffee porter from Austria, of all places, and sat down at a picnic table, trying to figure out what this might mean. Eventually I realized that Schneider's pass probably had more to do with its yeast than with its collaboration brew with Brooklyn Brewery. Instead of "craft beer" being used to mean "good beer" or even "hoppy beer," here the phrase seemed to mean "top-fermenting beer." There were certainly plenty of American hops — tons of Citra, Simcoe and Cascade — but not all of the beers there were super-hoppy. (Only about 95 per cent of them were.)

It was the yeast. Looking through my notes, I realized that almost every beer that day was made with *saccharomyces cerevisiae*, the traditional yeast used in Belgian and English — and thus American — ales. As far as I could tell, no beer that day was made with *saccharomyces pastorianus*, the so-called bottom-fermenting yeast that was traditionally used in German lager breweries. Of course, many of the big, industrial breweries like America's Budweiser and Miller made beer with *saccharomyces pastorianus*, but so did the most traditional, hand-crafted lagers from Bavaria. Those beers were probably excluded, I thought, because they did not fit the definition of craft beer for the festival organizers. Kathi-Bräu might mean craft beer to me, but that was not what craft beer meant in Berlin that particular afternoon. In that setting, at that time, craft beer must have meant something else.

I moved on, heading to the stand of one of the city's best young microbreweries, the maker of some wonderful hoppy ales which I had singled out in my *New York Times* article about beer in Berlin. The brewer himself was working the taps. I asked him for a pint of a beer I knew he was quite proud of. A moment later, he set the glass on the counter.

It didn't look like the pale ale I remembered, the one I had praised when I had written about his brewery earlier. This version of his beer was completely turbid, looking more like a soup than a beer, and when I tasted it it left a chalky, bitter back-bite from all the yeast.

I held it up and tried to peer through it, making a point of how cloudy it was. "I thought it looked different last time."

The brewer shook his head. "No, that's it," he answered. "Why?"

Perhaps it was the sun that day, or the work of tasting so many beers, or simply all the alcohol, but I was starting to feel like I was out of my element. The pale ale was disgusting, but if the brewer himself couldn't tell that, what was the point of me explaining it to him?

As the sun started to set on the festival, it was clear that the phrase *craft beer* didn't mean what I thought it meant, or at least not in Berlin. But could *craft beer* have come to mean "bad beer" instead?

The Meanings of Craft Beer, 2016

FROM *THE EPIC OF GILGAMESH*

Translated by C.F. Horne

Shamhat pulled off her clothing,
and clothed him with one piece
while she clothed herself with a second.
She took hold of him as the gods do
and brought him to the hut of the shepherds.
The shepherds gathered all around about him,
they marveled to themselves:
"How the youth resembles Gilgamesh —
tall in stature, towering up to the battlements over the wall!
Surely he was born in the mountains;
his strength is as mighty as the meteorite(!) of Anu!"
They placed food in front of him,
they placed beer in front of him;
Enkidu knew nothing about eating bread for food,
and of drinking beer he had not been taught.
The harlot spoke to Enkidu, saying:
"Eat the food, Enkidu, it is the way one lives.
Drink the beer, as is the custom of the land."

Enkidu ate the food until he was sated,
he drank the beer-seven jugs! — and became expansive and
    sang with joy!
He was elated and his face glowed.
He splashed his shaggy body with water,
and rubbed himself with oil, and turned into a human.

c. 2100 BC

MALT DOES MORE THAN MILTON CAN

A.E. Housman

Say, for what were hop-yards meant,
Or why was Burton built on Trent?
Oh many a peer of England brews
Livelier liquor than the Muse,
And malt does more than Milton can
To justify God's ways to man.
Ale, man, ale's the stuff to drink
For fellows whom it hurts to think:
Look into the pewter pot
To see the world as the world's not.
And faith, 'tis pleasant till 'tis past:
The mischief is that 'twill not last.
Oh I have been to Ludlow fair
And left my necktie God knows where,
And carried half-way home, or near,
Pints and quarts of Ludlow beer:
Then the world seemed none so bad,
And I myself a sterling lad;

And down in lovely muck I've lain,
Happy till I woke again.
Then I saw the morning sky:
Heigho, the tale was all a lie;
The world, it was the old world yet,
I was I, my things were wet,
And nothing now remained to do
But begin the game anew.

from "Terence, this is stupid stuff . . . ", *A Shropshire Lad*,
1896

JOLLY GOOD ALE AND OLD

William Stevenson

I cannot eat but little meat,
  My stomach is not good;
But sure I think that I can drink
  With him that wears a hood.
Though I go bare, take ye no care,
  I nothing am a-cold;
I stuff my skin so full within
  Of jolly good ale and old.
    Back and side go bare, go bare;
    Both foot and hand go cold;
    But, belly, God send thee good ale enough,
    Whether it be new or old.

I love no roast but a nut-brown toast,
  And a crab laid in the fire;

A little bread shall do me stead;
  Much bread I not desire.
No frost nor snow, no wind, I trow,
  Can hurt me if I wold;
I am so wrapp'd and thoroughly lapp'd
  Of jolly good ale and old.
    Back and side go bare, go bare, &c.

And Tib, my wife, that as her life
  Loveth well good ale to seek,
Full oft drinks she till ye may see
  The tears run down her cheek:
Then doth she trowl to me the bowl
  Even as a maltworm should,
And saith, "Sweetheart, I took my part
  Of this jolly good ale and old."
    Back and side go bare, go bare, &c.

Now let them drink till they nod and wink,
  Even as good fellows should do;
They shall not miss to have the bliss
  Good ale doth bring men to;
And all poor souls that have scour'd bowls
  Or have them lustily troll'd,
God save the lives of them and their wives,
  Whether they be young or old.
    Back and side go bare, go bare;
    Both foot and hand go cold;
    But, belly, God send thee good ale enough,
    Whether it be new or old.

1530?–1575

CAPTURING THE IMAGINATION

Charlie Papazian

Sometimes we get so caught up with our pride of "craft" beer we don't realize that our five senses — taste, smell, sight, hearing and touch — are not the final analysis of how we perceive beer. Yes, of course all of these senses weigh heavily in our decisions regarding the degree to which we like or dislike a beer. But it struck me after so many years of studying and proselytizing the art and science of beer evaluation that there is a higher value each and every individual considers when deciding what we enjoy in our lives.

I'm not a scholar. I don't have any degrees beyond my Bachelor of Science in Nuclear Engineering barely earned decades ago. No MBA, no marketing courses. Yes, I recall a course in metaphysics investigating the reasons "Why?" and graduate courses in, art, music, biomedical engineering and child psychology. I even recall a few Naval Science courses during my brief stint with the Navy ROTC. OK, I'll spill my beans at the risk of seeming naïve, never having taken courses in marketing: "image marketing" may be said to be about creating an image for a company, brand or product — right? But I think the word "image" could be applied to much more powerfully understanding the reasons why we actually make one choice over another. Imagination is a powerful factor that influences everything we perceive. It is at the heart of how we interpret our sense of taste, smell, hearing, sight and touch.

While judging beer I have wondered to what extent we should become detached from our imagination while evaluating beers. For brief moments I have become transfixed as it seemed we were machines trading data. The mechanics of human evaluation sometimes loses its lustre. No one noticed, but my eyes sometimes glaze over, though only briefly. But just as often the conversation would transform my glazed look to a lovely blue sky of hope and reality. Refreshingly, among the most veteran of beer evaluators (a.k.a. "judges") there is some element of reality mixed with the lustre of imagination finalizing most conversations. "The character in this beer, though some may consider it a technical flaw, is a real honest-to-God character found in some countryside breweries — and I like it." You can see the smile on a judge's face and a slight drift to the dream of some day recreating the experience, briefly now reliving the memory, the situation. The beer with its eccentric (not brewers' perfect) character had evoked imaginations and the warmth of the heart. The real reason we pay for beer.

I can recall days of pleasure and relaxation, simply by inhaling certain aromas. Cringe at the story I'm about to tell you, but it is strangely dear to me. I've often enjoyed one of my favourite British-style bitters on the rooftop of a favourite neighbourhood tavern. The view of the front range mountains, the warmth of the sun on early spring and late autumn days brought cheer. The all-malt full-flavoured draft bitter was easily sunstruck, but I've always continued to enjoy the whole event of being there. Now, I too realize how delightful it can be to succumb to one's imagination. Whenever I experience the aroma of an all-malt beer that is freshly sunstruck and slightly skunky, I smile and have come to not only enjoy these technically faulted beers, but would prefer it, because of the imagination and the warmth of heart it evokes. So have I gone nuts? Do you cringe and dismiss or do you stop and see what I'm trying to evoke? Sorry, but my imagination is all mine and there is no denying the power of where it can take me.

To "capture the imagination" is to legitimize our senses. And in being captured we hope it is in a positive sense. This is what we buy, isn't it? It's not all just an IPA that has 55 bittering units. Not just a stout that is 80 SRM, with a full-bodied creamy texture. Not only pale ale graced with Goldings and Fuggles hops. Not just barley wine or *doppelbock* with 9.14 per cent alcohol. Not a seasonal beer accented with nutmeg and orange peel. Nor are they all just brewed with the finest hop, malt, water and yeast. No, I don't really believe this is ultimately what we are seeking as beer drinkers of anything that matters to us. We see a label, we hear the name, our imagination takes us on a journey, a first contact, mini-seconds of processing our lifelong experiences. Our imagination takes over and then we decide. Will it be a good experience? Yes? I'll have one.

Beer drinker walks out of the store, six pack swinging at an arm's-length arc. The door closes behind and you know, you just know for sure, in fact we're positive, that if that beer has been well made, someone's imagination will transform all those beery characters into an experience so totally influenced by imaginations.

Is there any doubt? Smoked flavoured beer — it's a fringe example, but a good one. To many who try it for the first time it is "bacon." It evokes images of breakfast, and who would drink beer at breakfast? Or perhaps it is an awful experience with a smoke-filled memory, while to others it is the warmth of a convivial campfire or hearth-warming home fireplace. Imagination determines the decision to, at first, like or dislike. The point can be made for every other style of beer encountered to beer drinkers. Raspberry beers, apple beers, oatmeal stout, bitter, winter beer, spring beer, wheat beer: what goes on in the mind of first tastings of all the other beer styles with their unique flavours and character? Well, we know about American light lager: fun, young, lively, beautiful, sun, snow, mountains, freedom, things American; hopefully authentically American. Bang! There you have it — the imagination is taken care of.

But, sorry, though it may be successful for 93+% of all the beer enjoyed in the USA, my imagination takes me elsewhere. Why? Because I've offered myself to the opportunity to imagine my own great things. So what about all of those craft-brewed specialty beers?

What about them? 100+ styles and types of beers? Do we really believe for a moment that it's all about brewmasters, hops, malt, alcohol, colour, sweet and bitter? If so, we may be missing an opportunity — at least to evoke our imagination.

What about yours? Imaginations will alter every character you so either enjoy or, if you are a brewer, artfully created in your beer. So why not enjoy the imagination process, knowing that if you're part of it, perhaps you can help create or evoke a better image than beer, bacon and eggs in the morning? If you still can't quite imagine what it is I'm talking about, then sit down quietly with a beer and see where it REALLY takes you.

www.examiner.com, May 2016

Luminous As An Autumn Sunset

Thomas Hardy

In the liquor line Loveday laid in an ample barrel of Casterbridge "strong beer." This renowned drink — now almost as much a thing of the past as Falstaff's favourite beverage — was not only well calculated to win the hearts of soldiers blown dry and dusty by residence in tents on a hill-top, but of any wayfarer whatever in that land. It was of the most beautiful colour that the eye of an artist in beer could desire: full in body, yet brisk as a volcano; piquant, yet without a twang;

luminous as an autumn sunset; free from streakiness of taste; but, finally, rather heady. The masses worshipped it, the minor gentry loved it more than wine, and by the most illustrious county families it was not despised. Anybody brought up for being drunk and disorderly in the streets of its natal borough, had only to prove that he was a stranger to the place and its liquor to be honourably dismissed by the magistrates, as one overtaken in a fault that no man could guard against who entered the town unawares.

The Trumpet Major, 1880

SUCH HILARIOUS VISIONS

Edgar Allan Poe

Fill with mingled cream and amber,
I will drain that glass again.
Such hilarious visions clamber
Through the chambers of my brain.
Quaintest thoughts — queerest fancies,
Come to life and fade away:
What care I how time advances?
I am drinking ale today.

1848

ICE COLD IN ALEX

Christopher Landon

It was just six o'clock, too early for the usual drinking crowd and the bar was quite empty. It was just as the captain had said it would be; the high, marble-topped counter, the tall stools against it, the clean light room, the few tables grouped round the walls. After they had pushed through the swing door, they trooped up to the bar in silence, pulled out four stools and perched on them in a row. The barman yawned and got up from his seat to come forward and look at them without enthusiasm.

"Yes — ?" A pause, and then, "Sir."

"Set 'em up," said Anson.

"What up — ?"

Anson turned to Tom. "He thinks we're tramps. He thinks we can't pay. He's forgotten the order we put in six days ago." He fumbled in his pocket and produced two crumpled pound notes that he put on the counter.

"Get cracking, Joe. FOUR VERY, VERY, COLD RHEINGOLDS."

When they came up, again they were as he said they would be, pale amber, in tall thin glasses, and so cold, the dew had frosted on the outside before he put them down. They stood in a row now, but Tom waited, as he knew the others were waiting, for Anson to make the first move. He stared at his for a moment, looking all round it as if it were a rare specimen, then ran his finger up and down the side of the glass, leaving a clear trail in the dew. He said, "That's that," and lifted the glass and tilted it right back. Tom watched the ripple of the swallow in the lean throat, and there was a tight feeling inside him and his eyes were smarting and he knew that in a moment he would cry. So he lifted up his own glass and swallowed it fast.

When Anson put his glass down it was empty. "I quite forgot to drink your healths," he said. Then, to the barman, "Set 'em up again."

Ice Cold in Alex, 1957

CONTRIBUTORS AND ACKNOWLEDGEMENTS

Graham Greene (1904-1991) was related to the Greenes of Greene King. "A Pleasure That Has Never Failed Me", from *A Sort of Life* (1971), published by The Bodley Head and Vintage, is reprinted by permission of The Random House Group Limited.

Ernest Hemingway (1899-1961)'s greatest novels include *A Farewell to Arms* and *For Whom the Bell Tolls.*

Dale Jacquette (1953-2016) was Senior Professorial Chair in Theoretical Philosophy at the University of Bern. "Refreshing Like Truth Itself" is from *Beer and Philosophy*, © 2007 by Blackwell Publishing.

Mike Royko (1932-1997) was an American newspaper columnist for the *Chicago Daily News*, the *Chicago Sun-Times*, and the *Chicago Tribune*. "Brewed Through a Horse" is reprinted by permission of Sun-Times Media Productions, LLC.

Tom Acitelli is the author of *The Audacity of Hops: The History of America's Craft Beer Revolution* and writes regularly for *All About Beer* and FoodRepublic.com.

Maurice Healy (1887-1943) was an Irish lawyer and author whose books included *Slay Me With Flagons.*

Ian Nairn (1930-1983) was a writer, polemicist and broadcaster on architecture, and author of the classic *Nairn's London*. His love of pubs and beer is evident in his work. "The Best

Beers of Our Lives" and "The Charm of the Country Pub" are reprinted by permission of News UK and Ireland Limited.

Richard Jeffries (1848-1887) was an English nature writer and novelist whose works included *Bevis* and *After London*.

Roger Protz is editor of CAMRA's *Good Beer Guide*, author of many books including *The Ale Trail* and *300 Beers To Try Before You Die!*, and a forthright campaigner on many issues in the beer and pub trade.

Breandán Kearney was British Guild of Beer Writers Beer Writer of the Year 2015, Best Young Beer Writer 2015 and Best Beer and Food Writer 2015.

Dylan Thomas (1914-53) is best known for poems like "Do not go gentle into that good night" and his radio drama *Under Milk Wood*. "Its Brass-Bright Depths", from "Old Garbo" in *Portrait of the Artist as a Young Dog* (1940), published by Phoenix, is reproduced by permission of David Higham Ltd.

Byron Rogers's books include acclaimed biographies of the novelist and publisher J.L. Carr and the Welsh poet R.S. Thomas. He lives in Northamptonshire.

Ian Rankin's many novels include 21 featuring his popular detective Rebus. "Rebus on Draught", copyright © Ian Rankin, was published by *The Scotsman* in 2007 and is reproduced by permission of the author c/o Rogers, Coleridge & White Ltd, 20 Powis Mews, London WII IJN

Adrian Tierney-Jones writes for national newspapers and beer magazines from the *Sunday Times* Travel Magazine to

Original Gravity. His books include *1001 Beers You Must Try Before You Die* and *Britain's Beer Revolution*.

Charles Dickens (1812-1870) remains one of the best-loved authors in the English language.

Boak & Bailey has been the pen-name of Ray Newman and Jessica Slack since 2007, and the title of their popular blog. Some portions of "Becky's Dive Bar" appeared in modified form in their first book, *Brew Britannia* (Aurum Press, 2014), about the renaissance of British beer.

Patrick Hamilton (1904-62) was an English novelist and playwright who found fame with plays like *Rope* and *Gaslight*. His novels are renowned for their evocations of pub life. "This Cave of Refreshment", from his most famous novel *Hangover Square*, copyright © Patrick Hamilton, 1941, is reprinted by permission of A.M. Heath & Co. Ltd.

John Moore (1907-1967)'s trilogy of books about the English landscape includes *A Portrait of Elmbury*, from which "Roadhouse and Bar Parlour" is taken. Reprinted by permission of Peters Fraser and Dunlop (www.petersfraserdunlop.com) on behalf of the Estate of John Moore.

Fyodr Dostoyevsky (1821-1881) wrote some of the greatest Russian novels, including *Crime and Punishment* and *The Brothers Karamazov*.

Hilaire Belloc (1870-1953), born in France, became part of a literary generation including H.G. Wells and George Bernard Shaw. The extract from *This and That And The Other* is reprinted by permission of Peters Fraser and Dunlop (www.petersfraserdunlop.com) on behalf of the Estate of Hilaire Belloc.

Matthew Curtis is a regular contributor to *Good Beer Hunting* and *Ferment* magazine as well as his own blog Total Ales.

George Orwell (1903-1950)'s classic body of novels, essays and journalism includes *1984* and *Down and Out in Paris and London*. "The Moon Under Water", copyright © George Orwell, 1946, is reprinted by permission of Bill Hamilton as the Literary Executor of the Estate of the Late Sonia Brownell Orwell.

Pete Brown is one of Britain's foremost beer writers and author of many books including *Hops & Glory*, *Shakespeare's Local* and most recently *The Pub*.

Robert Louis Stevenson (1850-1894) was the author of *Treasure Island* and *The Strange Case of Dr Jekyll and Mr Hyde*.

Jaroslav Hašek (1883-1923) was a Czech writer, satirist and journalist. This extract from his most famous work, *The Good Soldier Švejk*, translated by Cecil Parrott (Penguin Classics, 2000; translation copyright © Cecil Parrott, 1973) is reproduced by permission of Penguin Books Ltd.

Simon Jenkins is a former Beer Writer of the Year and has been writing his Taverner column for the *Yorkshire Evening Post* since 1992. The second edition of his beer and pub guide *The Great Leeds Pub Crawl* was published in 2015.

Julian Symons (1912-1994) was an English writer and poet, best known for his crime novels. "Pub", copyright © Julian Symons 1943, is reproduced with permission of Curtis Brown

Group Ltd, London, on behalf of The Beneficiaries of the Estate of Julian Symons.

Mark Dredge is an award-winning beer, food and travel writer based in London. "Dad's Beer" is from *The Best Beer in the World* (Dog 'n' Bone Books, 2015).

Alastair Gilmour is the founder/editor of *Cheers* North East, the influential regional pubs magazine.

Jeff Evans is author of *The Good Bottled Beer Guide*, *CAMRA's Beer Knowledge* and *So You Want to Be a Beer Expert?* His writing can be found at www.insidebeer.com.

Stan Hieronymus has focused on all aspects of beer and brewing from monastic brewing to the future of indigenous American beers. He has written or co-written seven beer books, and blogs at www.appellationbeer.com.

Hugh de Selincourt (1878-1951)'s description of village cricket in *The Cricket Match* is a classic of its kind.

Richard Taylor focuses on the Scottish beer scene in his website The BeerCast, and now writes for BrewDog. Adam still visits the pub whenever he can.

Melissa Cole is acknowledged as one of the UK's leading beer and food experts. Author of *Let Me Tell You About Beer*, she is a beer consultant to various restaurants.

Garrett Oliver is the brewmaster of the Brooklyn Brewery as well as the highly regarded author of *The Brewmaster's Table*. He also edited *The Oxford Companion to Beer*.

Sir Walter Besant (1836-1901) was a novelist and historian who wrote mainly on London.

Graham Swift's celebrated novels include *Waterland*, *Last Orders* and *The Light of Day*. "About Coronation Ale" from *Waterland*, copyright © Graham Swift 1983, is reproduced by permission of A P Watt at United Agents on behalf of Graham Swift.

James Joyce (1882-1941) was the author of *Ulysses*, *A Portrait of the Artist as a Young Man* and *Finnegans Wake*.

Frank Priestley spent 20 years in the brewing industry, eventually becoming head brewer of Castle Eden in the north-east of England.

Jeff Alworth's books include *The Beer Bible* and the forthcoming *The Secrets of Master Brewers*. He lives in Portland, Oregon.

Joe Stange is author of *Around Brussels in 80 Beers*, co-author (with Tim Webb) of *Good Beer Guide to Belgium* and contributing editor for the American magazine *Draft*.

Stephen Beaumont's eleven books about beer include *The Beer & Food Companion* (2015) and, with Tim Webb, the now-landmark *World Atlas of Beer*. He travels the world extensively hosting beer dinners and directing tutored tastings from São Paulo to Helsinki.

Randy Mosher is an American beer writer whose works include *Tasting Beer*, *Radical Brewing* and *Beer For All Seasons*.

Simon Johnson (1969-2013) was a beer blogger and writer and is still missed by those who read his irreverent blog The Reluctant Scooper.

Patrick Leigh Fermor (1915-2011) is now regarded as one of Britain's best travel writers. "A Bavarian Tavern", from *A Time of Gifts* © Patrick Leigh Fermor 1977, is reproduced by permission of Hodder and Stoughton Limited.

John Holl is a journalist, the editor of *All About Beer* Magazine and author of several books including *The American Craft Beer Cookbook*.

Professor X. Landerer (1809-1885) was a German-born pharmacist and one of the first Professors in the University of Athens.

George Borrow (1803-1881) was an English author whose most famous books, about his travels around the United Kingdom and Europe, include *Wild Wales and* The *Romany Rye*.

Brian Glover's many books including *The World Encyclopedia of Beer* (1997) and *The Lost Beers and Breweries of Britain* (2012).

Will Hawkes contributes to national newspapers and is the author of *Craft Beer London* and *Beer: From Hop to the Perfect Pour*.

Emile Zola (1840-1902) is one of the greatest novelists in French literature.

Martyn Cornell is Britain's leading historian of beer and author of *Amber Gold & Black*, a history of British beer styles. He blogs at www.zythophile.co.uk.

Paul Theroux is an American travel writer and novelist whose works include *The Mosquito Coast* and *The Great Railway Bazaar*.

"Christmas Eve in Malawi", from *Jungle Lovers*, copyright © Paul Theroux 1971, is used by permission of The Wylie Agency (UK) Limited.

G.K. Chesterton (1874-1936) was a novelist, poet, dramatist and journalist whose most popular works were the Father Brown stories.

Elizabeth Craig (1883-1980) was a Scottish cookery writer who become one of the most influential in her field.

Lisa Morrison started a beer blog in 1997, long before anyone had even coined the term. She has hosted a regular local radio show about beer, is an active international beer judge, and has written for nearly every beer publication in the United States.

Arnold Bennett (1867-1931)'s novels include the acclaimed Clayhanger trilogy.

Lucy Saunders has written about the culinary appreciation of beer since 1988; her five cookbooks include *Dinner in the Beer Garden*. She lives in Milwaukee, Wisconsin. "Ale-Wyfes and Beer Chefs" is part of an essay that first appeared in *Beer Hunter, Whisky Chaser: New Writing on Beer and Whisky in Honour of Michael Jackson*, edited by Ian Buxton.

Sue Nowak edited all five editions of CAMRA's *Good Pub Food Guide*, is author of *The Beer Cook Book* and food writer for *Beer* magazine. She was the first woman chairman of the British Guild of Beer Writers.

Michael Jackson (1942-2007) Known as the Beer Hunter, Jackson was perhaps the first journalist to write about beer in a way that others wrote about music, wine, cinema and sport. His many books included *The Great Beers of Belgium* and *The World Guide to Beer*. "Now I Know Why they Call It The 'High' Table" is reprinted with thanks to Paddy Gunningham and Sam Hopkins.

Colin Dexter is the author of the Inspector Morse novels, and noted for his Hitchcock-like cameos in the hugely popular TV series. "Inspector Morse in the Pipes of Dawn", from *The Secret of Annexe 3*, © Colin Dexter 1986, is reproduced with permission of Pan Macmillan via PLSClear.

Robert Graves (1895-1985) is best known for his historical novels like *I, Claudius* and his memoir *Goodbye to All That*. "Strong Beer" is from *The Complete Poems in One Volume* (Carcanet Press Ltd, 2000).

Jonathan Meades is a writer, journalist and broadcaster, best known for his programmes on architecture. "Pint-Sized" is included in *Museum without Walls* (Unbound, 2013).

Thomas Mann (1875-1955) is one of the greatest German novelists who won the Nobel Prize for Literature in 1929. "A Good Glass of Porter" from *The Magic Mountain* by Thomas Mann, published by Martin Secker & Warburg Ltd, is reprinted by permission of The Random House Group Limited.

Evan Rail's books and ebooks include *Why Beer Matters* and *Good Beer Guide: Prague and the Czech Republic*. He lives in Prague.

A.E. Housman (1859-1936) was an English poet and scholar best remembered for his series of poems *A Shropshire Lad*.

William Stevenson (1530–1575) was an English clergyman who also wrote plays.

Charlie Papazian is a pioneer of the American home-brewing scene and author of the best-selling *The Complete Joy of Home Brewing*. He also founded the Great American Beer Festival and the Association of Brewers and is currently president of the Brewers' Association.

Thomas Hardy (1840-1928) was a novelist and poet whose works, including *The Mayor of Casterbridge* and *Tess of the D'Urbervilles*, were set in his native Dorset.

Edgar Allan Poe (1809-1849)'s most famous works include "The Fall of the House of Usher" and "The Pit and the Pendulum".

Christopher Landon (1911-1961) wrote novels and screen-plays, including that for the classic film of *Ice Cold in Alex*. The extract from his novel *Ice Cold in Alex*, © Christopher Landon 1957, is reproduced by permission of The Orion Publishing Group, London.

Thanks also to John Holl at *All About Beer*, Erika Reitz at *Draft*, Rebecca Johnson, Tom Stainer and Claire-Michelle Taverner-Pearson at *Beer,* Joanne Potter at Merlin Unwin Books, Linda Kaplan and David Godwin.